SOME OF OUR PARTS

SOME OF OUR PARTS

WHY WE ARE MORE THAN THE LABELS WE LIVE BY

LAURA KENNEDY

eriu

First published in the UK by Eriu
An imprint of Black & White Publishing Group
A Bonnier Books UK company

4th Floor, Victoria House,
Bloomsbury Square,
London, WC1B 4DA

Owned by Bonnier Books
Sveavägen 56, Stockholm, Sweden

✕ – @eriu_books

⊙ – @eriubooks

Hardback – 978-1-80418-677-0
Ebook – 978-1-80418-678-7

A CIP catalogue of this book is available from the British Library.

Designed by IDSUK (Data Connection) Ltd
Printed and bound by Clays Ltd, Elcograf S.p.A.

3 5 7 9 10 8 6 4 2

Every reasonable effort has been made to trace copyright holders of material
reproduced in this book, but if any have been inadvertently overlooked
the publishers would be glad to hear from them.

Eriu is an imprint of Bonnier Books UK
www.bonnierbooks.co.uk

For Emma, who showed me that there is more than one way,
and because we keep our promises

Contents

Introduction

The people [of England] think themselves free but they choose what is customary in preference to their inclination until it does not occur to them to have any inclination except for what is customary.

— John Stuart Mill, *On Liberty*

WHEN YOU'RE YOUNG AND not quite sure who you are, you might as well become a doctor if you can manage it. So I did. I became a doctor, but the wrong kind. Or the wrong kind to fulfil most parents' ambitions for their child. I'm the sort of doctor who, when someone begins to choke on a plane and the flight attendant wails in ululating panic, '*Is there a doctor on board?*' shrinks lower in their seat and turns up the volume on the objectively terrible 1990s action film they're enjoying. I can't tell you about the anatomy of your throat or the mechanics by which your face is presently going purple as an oversized grape drains the oxygen from your brain and the life from your body. I could tell you what Aristotle has to teach us about what constitutes a good life, but given the scenario, that might just seem like rubbing it in a bit. Philosophers aren't always welcomed with open arms, even if someone isn't currently losing their battle for life to the crimson seedless stubbornly lodged in their windpipe.

I'll tell you this much – nobody gazes into the cherubic face of their toddler and declares, 'I *do* hope she grows up to be a philosopher.' If they did say it, it could only be directed at a toddler against whom they had some sort of lifelong vendetta. Philosophers are odd people. They are a little bit sad (often in the melancholy sense of the word but also sometimes the 'lingering stiffly on the periphery of your cousin's wedding reception in a creased jacket that smells of cupboards' sense). They are the person at the birthday party wondering aloud over the people singing 'Happy Birthday' whether Larry the golden retriever has a soul. Meanwhile, Larry has never looked happier than he does in this moment of the utterly contented life in which he seems always wholly present and invested, apparently presuming that it is him for whom everyone is singing. And why not? Everyone should be singing for Larry. He's living the good life, whether or not Aristotle would agree (and he wouldn't). Most of us might choose to be Larry rather than the philosopher. So what I'm getting at is this: I'm not that kind of doctor. I can't treat your rash but I can ruin your birthday party.

This is a story I tell myself, and now you, about who philosophers are, and who I am. But how accurate is it? It's quite one-dimensional. It's a partial perspective. For one thing, I wouldn't ruin your birthday party. It's far more likely that I simply wouldn't turn up in the first place. I'd get stressed about what to wear and recall (with my head in my hands) the last birthday party I attended when I found myself standing next to an unfamiliar man by a table covered in mildly disappointing peanut butter apple wedges and Capri Suns. The birthday girl was turning four. Total silence seemed odd under the circumstances so I offered him a blackcurrant flavour and said 'Good to meet you. So are you afraid of death?' in an attempt to make conversation. He looked deeply uncertain as to whether I was threatening him and, in hindsight, I do see where he was coming from.

Even Larry's presence wouldn't tempt me to your party. You might invite me regardless (a kind though bad call, if you ask me, but it's your day) and think, when I don't attend, that I'm unsociable. Maybe rude. You might layer this analysis atop more general expectations around how someone like me (as you see it) should behave. This is how we navigate the world. We construct models of reality through experience, and we consider ourselves and other people through these models.

In that fluid, easy way she had of effortlessly scooping up a profound truth and cradling it gently in the palm of her hand without killing it, the writer Joan Didion pointed out the narrative vehicle of these models, suggesting that we understand reality by building it through stories. She wrote in *Slouching Towards Bethlehem* that 'we tell ourselves stories in order to live'. We arrange reality as we see it but in doing so we both construct the story and reify it. There is an extent to which we make the world through the act of describing it. This is the best method human beings know of fumbling our way through, as we all must. To get anything done, it seems we have to make a few presumptions and then build upon them. Only philosophers at birthday parties have time to reconsider first principles and it's not a job people are lining up for.

This inferential, gradual story-building is how, along with the input of other people (some of which we consent to and some we don't), the stories that represent us both internally and out in the world are created. It is the means by which our families and communities tell us who we are, for better and worse, from the moment we are born. It's why you can't escape the version of yourself your mother decided is your personality when you were sixteen, or why your friend keeps giving you owl-themed gifts because you once said in passing, fifteen years ago, that owls seem cool but now you can't disabuse her and you're both apparently just in this forever. It's why you'll see the person your boyfriend dumped you for at school twenty years later and think 'tramp', as though their entire personhood, past and future, is characterised by one long-gone moment in your life and despite your deep understanding that your boyfriend was an ass. It's why a

4

significant part of me can never fully absorb the idea that my brother is a dad with responsibility for two human lives. It's tough to get past my memory of him routinely smashing chocolate teacakes into his forehead at speed before eating them and declaring an intention to be a hippo when he grows up. It's why he'll never entirely take anything I say or think seriously because he remembers the time I absentmindedly pooed myself, aged four, while intently focused on trying to play the neighbours' out-of-tune piano.

The stories we live by are richly layered. The most fundamental ones lie so deep beneath our beliefs and choices that most of the time we don't even realise they're there. But they are we why we can never quite shake the cruel things the school bully told us about ourselves, and why when we are young, we believe our parents to be objective when they tell us we are clever or stupid, weak or resilient, pretty or ugly. We add to these inherited and socialised stories in order to make and remake ourselves over time: the bundle of concepts, ideas and behaviours that are 'me'; what the philosopher Gilbert Ryle called 'the ghost in the machine'. The confluence of performed behaviours and beliefs that mark our individual path through the world and render us distinct from all the other ghosts engaged in the same business.

We live in a time in which we are routinely expected to hold two conflicting beliefs without appearing to be overly bothered by the dissonance. It feels a bit like the intellectual equivalent of patting the top of your head while rubbing your stomach in circular motions. Except you have to do it as the world burns around you, everyone on the internet is desperately seeking validation from everyone else while pretending they're suddenly an epidemiologist or a historian of the Middle East and wearing a bikini that some fast-fashion brand sent them for free without disclosing it. And you're thinking about that song by Irish comedian David O'Doherty, 'Life'. The one in which he rests a silly little keyboard on his knees and looks touchingly relatable and vulnerable while he sings, *'Life is a marathon, not a sprint. But it's a sort of marathon that you have to sprint. And there's hurdles and weights to lift. And cycling and archery. Life is basically the Olympics but at the end you don't get a medal, you die.'*

We are collectively consumed by individuality but routinely seek ourselves within the confines of group identity. 'Who am I?' we go about asking mirrors, Gilbert Ryle, Larry the retriever, strangers at parties and the internet at large, until someone (usually online) appears on our timeline with what might be as good an answer as any. Usually one that takes the form of some sort of one-dimensional or overtly politicised approach to self-help. Someone who creates a meme misquoting the Stoic philosopher Epictetus, who I'm confident never actually said 'Cut those toxic bitches out of your life, Queen.'

We declare ourselves to one another across the digital ether, and increasingly in the material world, labels first. Gender labels. Labels that suggest the ethnic or cultural groups we belong to. Labels indicating our nationality, sexuality and political leaning. Family labels. Professional labels. We list them like our components. As though these are the parts that add up to the central story of who we are. Except labels are tools, as useful as we make them. We can use them to open a door or to bash a head in, depending on how we are inclined to think about them.

In her book *At the Same Time: Essays and Speeches*, Susan Sontag wrote, 'Generally a moral principle is something that puts one at *variance* with accepted practice. And that variance has consequences, sometimes unpleasant consequences, as the community takes its revenge on those who challenge its contradictions.' The same goes for asserting individual identity in the context of collective expectation. We all carry labels. You're a woman, a man, a solicitor tripping in a dirty puddle on his walk into work, a toxic bitch, a socially incompetent dolt accidentally threatening people at a birthday party. Sometimes we conflate these labels with our identity at large, or others do, so that we forget the possibility of a self that is larger and more complex than the lens through which we are granted one limited view.

John Stuart Mill is the philosopher so currently beloved by everyone from your annoying, slightly overzealous political activist friend to effective altruist neo-Utilitarian tech bros in San Francisco determined to figure out definitive answers to philosophical questions in their effort to save the world by the next fiscal quarter. We won't hold all that against Mill himself, whose work was so foundational to the society we now live in. It has value for more people than those who ask Chat GPT to summarise the main ideas Dostoevsky explores in *The Brothers Karamazov* so they can 'solve the novel for X real quick' over a protein-rich lunch. In our time, we voraciously strive to stand out as unique individuals, but strictly within the bounds of group fealty and conformity. We want to be exceptional as long as we fit in.

It turns out that Mill observed much the same about his own society. In his 1859 essay 'On Liberty', one of the most robust and celebrated defences of individual identity and free expression ever written, Mill wrote that 'in our time, the yoke of law has become lighter but the yoke of opinion has become heavier.' He might have been referring to anything from your company Slack channel to that post you redrafted seven times to ensure it wouldn't provoke the cleansing fire of social media puritans and get you cancelled. Mill was concerned by the power of civil society – not the laws we create but the norms we live by – to limit individual freedom. At the Stanford Humanities Center in 2016 the intellectual historian Quentin Skinner delivered a lecture entitled 'A Genealogy of Liberty'. In it, he suggested that this limitation of the individual as Mill saw it occurs through implicit pressure towards conformity with conventions of behaviour dictated by the society in which we live. Skinner said, 'Mill thinks that where that demand is very strong, as he thought it was in 19th-century Britain, then the effect will be to cause you inauthentically to internalise those social norms until you follow them in preference to your authentic desires.'

In other words, we internalise the dominant narrative about how best to live within society, and before we realise it, we cease to exercise our own judgement. Worse, we cease to be able to identify our own judgement from that of the collective. This outsourcing of judgement to the collective is why we feel so deeply conspicuous when our choices or beliefs don't coincide with those of the people around us. Big picture, it's why most people can't seem to tell the difference between ethics and law. Closer to home, it's why you might feel pressure to get married by a certain stage in your life, or to have a child even if you're unsure whether parenthood is for you, or to post that unrealistically flattering photo to Instagram rather than the one that actually looks like you most of the time.

Mill suggests that instead of exercising our own judgement (ethical or otherwise) we reproduce the standards of those around us as if they are our own and in so doing elevate them to objectivities. We follow trends in the belief that there must be something objectively valuable about them if it looks like everyone around us agrees that this is the case. That's why every woman who was a teenager in the nineties still can't grow eyebrows and why millennials will still insist, when pushed, that blink-182 were actually kind of okay if you were there at the time. It's also how Gen Z has been tricked into thinking that low-rise trousers can be made to work even though the results first time round scarred a generation. It's why everyone's house extension seems to feature the same open-plan kitchen in one of three colours. It's why we make choices that we sometimes don't really even want to make but which seem like the obvious next step, the most desirable option, or the fastest route to status, praise and acceptance.

We defer to the majority view on social, ethical (and other) questions without noticing that our perspective conveniently so often matches the dominant one within our culture. We absorb the aesthetics and the morality and the politics. We absorb and reproduce the status quo. According to Skinner, 'people – this is Mill's point – are not reflecting on their choices and if you don't stand back in this Socratic way that he always asks you to do from your choices, then they're not genuinely free choices because you're simply allowing the circumpressures of your society to dictate what you think are your choices.'

The famous Miranda Priestly 'cerulean' monologue from *The Devil Wears Prada* probably wasn't intending to channel Mill on liberty, though it does and I'm delighted about that. Priestly, the infamous fashion magazine editor played by Meryl Streep, casually decimates Andrea Sachs, played by Anne Hathaway, a conflicted assistant working at *Runway* as a means to an end while maintaining elitist aspirations towards 'real' journalism. Sachs disdains her job and what seems to her the snobby, shallow industry that created it (we're all hypocrites).

Priestly upbraids Sachs for chuckling as the editor contemplates a choice between two blue belts, her assistant scoffing sniffily that the two 'look exactly the same' to her. 'I'm still learning about this stuff . . .' Sachs says. Priestly fires her a withering look and explains the origin of this particular cerulean shade – the one that gave rise to 'that lumpy blue sweater' worn by Sachs in the scene – among various designers' collections.

In her devastatingly flat, iron-velvet voice, the editor tells Sachs that the 'lumpy blue sweater' she is wearing is the trickledown outcome of decisions made in the room where they stand and the industry that they are part of. It is not an entirely free choice.

Sachs made the error of presuming that the rejection of one in-group identity is a form of identity itself, that by establishing what we are not, we in some way positively assert what we are by default. There's a lot of that going around at the moment. She fell into the error that Mill describes in the earlier Quentin Skinner quote and failed to reflect on her own choice (both of the beliefs that she holds around

11

fashion and journalism, and in her selection of one lumpy blue sweater). Sachs had presumed hers to be a free choice made independently of the systems in which she lives. Priestly disabused her of that idea.

Everything is more than it seems, and so are we. Even this book. The cover reproduces patterns you're already familiar with to let you know whether it was written for someone like you. To give you a sense of what you're dealing with, it contextualises the book within an identity category, and that category is, vaguely: non-fiction books on culture and life by women, for people, mainly women, who are interested in that stuff. It's designed to signal 'this may be a bit like these other books you might know and like' in the hope that you will pick it up. That you will recognise something of your own identity as you understand it reflected in the design and, in this world of infinite choice, tax returns, missed calls from your mother and birthday parties you're not being invited to, decide it's worth taking a chance on.

We evaluate one another in similar ways, funnelling the unique complexity of every person we encounter – and ourselves – through the mental model of the world we've built throughout our lives, and labelling them. There is irony, then, in the idea that the cover of *Some of Our Parts* must signal one particular kind of identity while the pages within express scepticism about how far such labels can ever really take us. Whether they can ever capture us in our fullness, our complexity, and our inherent contradiction. The label is never the full story. It can't be.

We carry so many identities during our lifetime, each one with an attendant label that we wear out in the world. Some we choose of our own volition. Others are forced on us and we can either fight or embrace them. These identities tell us stories about ourselves. Stories that we use, as Didion said, to live. To make a life. To construct a self that we perform in the world. A version of ourselves that we can recognise and put words to when we look in the mirror. But there is no real individuality without agency. Without autonomy – the choices we make for ourselves without deference to collective judgement or passing trends, the elements of identity that we choose to embrace or eschew as Mill suggested, in a Socratic way – we cannot really be ourselves. We can only be a version performed for the benefit of others. A reproducer of norms. Someone with 'no inclination except for what is customary'. In short, someone who is not an individual at all but a person masquerading as one.

I am not for an instant suggesting, like Andrea Sachs, or your adolescent self (no judgement – it's a rite of passage), that friction itself constitutes a meaningful or valid identity. It doesn't. Complaining about things might be a personality type in the online landscape we all float through, but it isn't one in the material world – it makes for a cheerless, coercive person. You won't find a constructive, rich individual identity simply by knowing what you're not, or in reaction to what you're not. That is not a self. It's a not-self. Building an identity primarily in opposition to things we hate or disdain makes for an even worse party guest than a philosopher. As the cultural commentator Ayishat Akanbi puts it, 'anyone selling you an enemy is also selling you a master'.

To be ourselves is to accept that there are ways in which we will depart from the mean and resist the pressure to fall in line when we don't freely choose to for reasons we can respect and justify to ourselves. It is to embrace the culture we come from, the family that loves us, to connect with the community we live in without compromising ourselves. It is to wear the social, political, diagnostic and other labels we might pick up or have pinned to us as we go through our lives insofar as we see the value in doing so. It is to decide what we think and who we are by stepping back, as Mill suggested, Socratically. It is to question rather than passively to absorb. To decide rather than solely to be told.

I'll tell you this right now – the answers aren't in here. I haven't got the vaguest idea how to solve the major cultural and political drift that can leave so many of us uncertain of who we are in a world we increasingly don't fully recognise. Like the philosopher nobody likes inviting, I only know how to ask questions. The answers are up to you. I'm not offering a six-week self-actualisation retreat in a French Riviera resort that you can buy at the approximate cost of your child's college education and your best lung. I'm not offering anything but questions. I'm not even coming to your birthday party. But questions do have value, especially in a time of mass confusion when, more than ever before, the sum of the labels attached to a person who carries them is constantly mistaken for the totality of who they are and who they are permitted to be.

I have worn a lot of labels, by choice and otherwise. Here, I consider the ones I've picked up, rejected, lost, had stuck to my back like a 'kick me' poster in the schoolyard at lunchtime, worn for a while and lost connection to. In its way, each one makes a discrete claim on who I am, as the labels you bear do for you. Each one is a means of translating who we are to the world and, when seen as the most important or true element of who we are, shrinking and flattening us. Each one is part of the story, nothing more.

At various points in my life I've been an unwilling philosopher at a birthday party, a beauty editor hyperventilating in a cupboard while waiting for a world-famous celebrity to phone me, a completely unequipped daughter watching her mother die, an Irish person who complains about Ireland, an Irish person who loves Ireland, one half of an interracial relationship, a suspicious woman with a brand-new autism diagnosis in her thirties, a baffled working-class kid struggling at an elite university, a person who lives next door to a drug dealer and has no furniture, a teenager with no hair, suddenly illiterate, an emigrant, the granddaughter of a woman who's just been sectioned, the daughter of an alcoholic, a writer, a badly behaved child, someone who apparently had the worst wedding ever, and nobody's mother. Also a houseplant enthusiast but I'm not sure how critical that one is.

The wonderful thing about all of us is that who we are is something informed by but ultimately beyond all of it. We are something that emerges, miraculous and impossible to capture in its totality, like the ghost in the machine, from somewhere beyond our component parts or the language that we use to capture and convey them. We are something ineffable. Something more.

1

Feminist

It had seemed as close as a star to the moon. Now it was again a green light on a dock. His count of enchanted objects had diminished by one.
                    – F. Scott Fitzgerald, *The Great Gatsby*

IT'S NINE O'CLOCK AT NIGHT and I am sitting inside a cupboard. The cupboard is tucked like a confessional or an elevator deep within the pounding ribcage of a high-rise building in the heart of London. As I sit, panicking quietly, a single glacial rivulet of sweat trickles down my spine, fingernail sharp. It's been a long day and I ate some questionably dated crackers that I found in my bag for dinner. I've come in here for some privacy, ostensibly to wait for a phone call from one of the most famous women on earth but I'm using the downtime till then to rethink the trajectory of my entire career and engage in a quick spot of existential crisis.

For more than six years now I have, among my other jobs, worked as a beauty editor – writing and commissioning articles on beauty for magazines and newspapers, mostly big-name broadsheets, first in Ireland and now in London. The job has allowed me to indulge my enduring enthusiasm for beauty – everything about it fascinates me, from the delicious sensoriality and the artistry to the psychology and sociology of it. The way it can transform people into living art or change the way other people respond to them. The status that proximity to beauty standards affords people. The things for which we instinctively consider beauty to be a proxy – health, wealth, influence. The way that it lubricates a woman's route through the world, unjust though that may be.

It is largely a female-dominated industry and has been a powerful means of connecting me with other women. It is also a haven for affable, creative weirdos. The sort of people I've always been drawn to. Those who I couldn't imagine ever tolerating an office job and who wouldn't want one. It's an industry that contains all sorts of women – from accomplished doctors and chemists to astonishingly gifted creatives, beloved and not-so-beloved celebrities, selachian entrepreneurs, status-hungry it-girls, egotists and grifting wellness nuts.

While people at the very top are often male, beauty is an industry valued at $626 billion in 2024 and is mostly run by women. It is an often-overlooked example of the dynamics created within a female-dominated hierarchy. We are all steeped in cultural conversation on what the world might look like if it were largely run by women – we already have an example in the beauty industry and while it's a thriving and exciting area of work whose operation is radically different from male-dominated areas I've worked in, it's not a utopia.

The move I have made from Irish beauty journalism to its UK counterpart is one that few people successfully manage and I know that it is envied at home. On press trips with UK media, the Irish were traditionally ignored as provincial outliers. There is a very palpable hierarchy, and I've climbed several rungs higher up on it than where I formerly dangled. I feel the 'how did she manage that?' energy radiating from former colleagues, and I get it. An exceptional boss gave me an opportunity when she had no reason to. Like most good things that have happened to me, this appears to be a frustrating confluence of luck, good timing and pretending I have the competence to do a thing until I actually develop the competence to do it. I'm very grateful but riddled by the sense that I've crossed over into some alternative timeline where I may not belong.

In an industry obsessed by status, the knowledge that I'm perceived as successful by the people I came up with in journalism gives something petty in me a minor thrill. Until I remember that I am hunched over, exhausted and sweating, in a cupboard, having been casually told to cancel any plans I might have tonight. The person I am waiting for would be recognisable in pretty much any country on earth and is widely considered the epitome of aspirational elegance and entrepreneurial accomplishment.

As this day has progressed, the demands coming in from her PR team have become increasingly insane. This is standard enough – major celebrities can be very affable and polite in person because they hire experts in pushy powerplay to engage in the less pleasant elements of public image insulation on their behalf. Someone has to protect their interests, and they'll look self-interested if they do it themselves. The emails stream in through the afternoon, each biting snippily at the heels of the last, each ratcheting up my escalating stress levels marginally higher. First, the call is coming in at 4 p.m. Then it's six. She's running behind, so we'll do it at eight. Something has come up, so we'll have to cancel. We'll do it tomorrow. Maybe next Wednesday if she has time. Fifteen minutes later: actually, does tonight at nine work? You can have twenty-five minutes. Twenty minutes. Fifteen minutes. Five minutes. Actually, twenty minutes. No pressure but send us your questions in advance. Also, we'd like to see the article before it runs. Also, we'd like approval rights over the final draft (these two are always refused by any magazine or newspaper, and they ask in the knowledge that they will certainly be refused now. Still, it's worth a go.) Also, here are the topics you absolutely cannot under any circumstances bring up in your questions.

My editor rushes by. She is small and quick, whirring about with a hummingbird energy and her efficiency frightens me. She stops momentarily with a rustle of weighty Chanel fabric, draping everyone in the fragrance of understated affluence (also Chanel) and says in rushed, merry tones, 'Put her age in the copy!'

She sniffs gently, nosing out the opportunity (she's good at this – it is why she is a career editor). '*And ask her what feminism means for her now and if that's changed since the nineties.*'

'Ooh yes, that's good!' The voice of another female editor a few desks down loops over my head and in through my reluctant ears. 'That's good.' She waves a finger as if to say, *Feminism is so relevant.*

'And motherhood! How she juggles it all. Oh and of course be sure to ask her about the weight thing! That's critical,' my editor says, though by now I can only see the back of her glossy silk blouse as it rounds the corner. 'See if you can get something new there.'

I look down at the list of forbidden topics the PR team has sent over. The first item on it is, unsurprisingly, the weight thing. Slightly lower down is a proviso that the celebrity's age is not to be referenced or asked about.

A metal band is tightening around my chest. I'm perfectly conscious that this interview is a major get. A very big deal. What it really is, is a test. To see if I can be trusted with something like this again. If I can winkle out an exciting headline. It should be handled with maximum tact. (I'm not particularly tactful.) I'll need to do that journalist thing of affably and by indirection drawing from this woman things she absolutely does not intend to tell me. (I'm not good at this and I'd prefer not to get good at it.) These pieces of her life or thoughts will provide fodder for a headline which will make the publication money and help maintain its prestige. They will elevate my own status and ensure I get more work of this kind. This is media. This is how it works.

Except I don't want to ask this woman about her weight or how she manages doing it all. Partially because I don't care but also because I don't want to write something that will make the world a little bit worse. But this is the game. She has vast, high-level media training to wend her way through my questions without revealing a single thing that isn't helpful to her brand, even from an exquisite hotel in LA as I sit here in a cupboard, listening to the spaces between her words. Between plugs for the beauty product bearing her endorsement, because celebrities only talk to journalists like me when they have units to shift.

I must hang on the line, nosing like a hyena, betraying no desperation or self-interest, and sniff out any opportunity for a get. It's the game. We both know it. She, a massively successful and wealthy celebrity, never seems to lose energy for it but then it keeps her in the life she enjoys. I, a journalist on a temporary contract who skipped dinner, kind of hate this. I am depressed by the disingenuous conversation we have.

I detest the one-dimensional fiction of ideal woman-hood and family life that is being portrayed, and the expectation that I should disseminate it. People can only read about it and either dismiss it entirely or feel bad about their own complex and nuanced lives in comparison; about their imperfect bodies and their kitchen drawer that they never get around to tidying and their ordinary children who don't wear Gucci. I've done my research and can tell that this woman I'm speaking with is clearly vastly more complex and interesting than the sanitised sliver of human press release she is offering me here in this brief conversation. I want to at least try to maintain some level of personal integrity. Only here in this cramped cupboard, I can't seem to find it.

The resulting interview is a lost opportunity. I know this. It's boring. It contains nothing sensational, contro-versial or particularly attention-grabbing. I didn't ask about the weight thing. I knew what would happen as a result of that choice but I couldn't bear to do it. I did reference her age. It's publicly available information. Publicists are paid to manufacture alternative realities, including ones where they're the person who decides what goes into the article. In the end, I emerge from the cupboard, crumpled, with stale cracker dust festooning my collar, and write it up as best I can under the circum-stances, in a futile attempt to balance completely conflicting imperatives. The resulting interview doesn't run and is resigned to the can as a failed effort.

Having arrived in London around a year before the cupboard interview, and still being new to the workings of UK media, I have been slowly grappling with a strange, rising dissonance. Here I am in the cultural omphalos, inside women's media, the means by which academia and literature filter down into middle-class consciousness and beyond. I am a beauty editor during the very last hurrah of magazines. In the stoic, soldiering-on phase of moribundity. Edward Enninful is still editor of British *Vogue*. Major women's magazines still have budgets, if shrinking ones, as advertisers and brands are just beginning the pivot to prioritise the reach and power of social media and influencer investment.

But we're not dead yet. I've recently commissioned a major name for £2 a word, vaguely the equivalent of Carrie Bradshaw's fictional and astonishing $4 a word for *Vogue* in *Sex and the City*, a sum that had every writer I know nauseated with covetousness, crippling inadequacy and the collective sense that we are all in fact utterly doomed. But not quite yet. The pandemic, which will see many magazines fold or restructure and the beauty industry having to rapidly reorient itself, is over a year away. The magazine editors I work under are the last breed of Miranda Priestly, Anna Wintour types. They live in London townhouses, on salaries vastly beyond anything my generation could conceive of, and they are unquestioned rulers within their own fiefdoms, though the ceiling is beginning to crack above their heads. Everyone can feel it, they can feel it, and the atmosphere is changing as a result. The industry is in big trouble. We're all in trouble. Trouble makes everything slightly less chic.

Meanwhile, in this female-dominated environment, pretty much every woman around me identifies as a feminist. They feature plus-size models in magazines and publicly describe fat activism as empowering, but when I meet them at work events they're always on a diet or stressing about fitting into the tiny clothing samples that brands send them to court favour. Nobody eats the bread that sits in the centre of the table. Thinness is actively and vocally lionised among the tastemakers around me, but this is not overtly reflected directly in anything that is published. Some describe marriage as archaic, patriarchal and unnecessary, but most colleagues over thirty-five are married. We write articles and make social media content about the best tips for wedding make-up that lasts all day.

Non-motherhood is championed in writing as an enlightened, environmentally conscious or valid choice, but most women around me either already have children or talk openly about their plans to have them. It's the same sense of friction that I feel when I scroll through social media. There is constant talk of empowerment, breaking with tradition, radical self-acceptance and rejection of social pressure and yet within the actual choices I see being made around me, the usual trajectory reflected is marriage, home ownership, and then

25

motherhood. There is nothing at all wrong with this – I've happily engaged in two of the three – but when it comes to feminism, so many women appear to be saying one thing and doing another, or rather claiming one set of values in theory and living another in practice. I'm struck by this and why it might be.

I'm conscious that I have been given access to the rooms that some women dream of being in. I've travelled all over the world funded by make-up, skincare and fragrance brands. I've taken a private tour of Coco Chanel's Paris apartment (that was a highlight), flown business class to New York and LA to interview celebrities or attend launch parties. I've gone on spa trips with some of the world's biggest influencers to destinations I couldn't afford to visit if I saved for three decades. I've wandered about backstage at fashion weeks and accidentally seen supermodels in their underwear, and had access to the best hair stylists, make-up artists, dermatologists and cosmetic doctors in the world. These are people whose job specifically involves the augmentation and maximisation of beauty. Where I have ended up could not be further from where I started. I consider that, sitting in the cupboard and waiting for the phone call to come in. Where I started.

*

I'm sixteen and have just had all my hair cut off. Or most of it. There are a couple of centimetres left, tufting resentfully from my scalp. While temporary style changes are all in good fun, the 'big haircut' is usually a signifier of one of two things in a girl's or woman's life: you're either announcing internal change, or you're making a declaration of intention to change. As I glance into the mirror, I consider that cutting off my hair is a deeply subversive and intellectual thing to do. Not heroic, necessarily, but pretty brave in a country and time in which female standards of beauty for young women are fixed and entail maintaining as much hair (on your head) as possible. My choice certainly confirms, my thoughts tell me, that I am a very different and interesting person. Possibly mysterious. Possibly when people see me now they will stop for a moment, arrested by how different and interesting I seem and think to themselves, *My goodness, that girl seems so mysterious.* I find myself hoping that they will think precisely this. Some acknowledgement would be nice. I am, after all, trying so desperately hard to be mysterious and interesting that I have just cut all my hair off. My knuckles are pinched white with effort.

The aesthetics of the cut won't help my case. The result is less 'Audrey Hepburn in *Roman Holiday*' or 'Winona Ryder in *Girl, Interrupted*' and more 'snap-on Lego man hair', but I live in the little Irish city of Limerick in the early 2000s. The world's most celebrated hair stylists do not live here. I doubt they've ever visited. I won't meet a great hair stylist or learn the alchemical, transformative skill they possess for another decade or so. Until then it's just me and my reachy and mysterious, if technically rudimentary and slightly desperate – in all senses of the word – pixie cut.

When I first walk into the salon with my mutinous Irish hair grazing the top of my backside, the stylist refuses to do what I'm asking. 'Oh no,' she says in the tone of an older female relative who can just say things without softening them up in any way first. 'That's a godawful idea, pet.' I'm quietly scandalised that she refers to me, a paying client who in fact walked thirty minutes to get here with my Walkman in my backpack, as 'pet'. 'Don't do it. You'll regret it. You'll be in tears, like. That's what always happens.'

I should perhaps consider this statement carefully as a potential reflection of the quality of service I'm about to receive rather than the general emotional instability of this woman's client base. But I'm sixteen, so everything she says feels like it's about me. Everything everyone says feels like it's about me.

I'm embarrassed by the rejection and not a little thrown off. How do you convince someone you don't know that you're qualified to make a decision like this? I bristle internally. Isn't it my hair? Haven't I grown it myself from this scalp she sees before her? I'm the kind of person who makes bold decisions. Or I'd like to be, and this haircut might just be the key to all of it. It certainly feels very important that I walk out of here a completely different person.

I promise the stylist that I've carefully considered the move for a while. I say it casually, as though I take big life decisions like this all the time, but also quietly, because I'm mysterious. No boy has broken my heart and prompted a spiral into masochistic self-mutilation. I'm not trying to prove a point to my mother (though I am and she's thwarted that by thoroughly supporting my radical decision, rendering it distinctly less radical). It's not because my dad left (though he did, but I'm not telling this random hair stylist my business). I'm simply doing what you do when you're a teenager. I'm trying on selves to find a fit. I have no substantial, confident idea who I am or how I might go about discovering this information, so I'm giving near-baldness a go because you have to start somewhere. I want to shock myself, and the world around me, into change.

Next month, I'll start a new school after years of extended misery and profound loneliness at my old one. This is the first real change I have experienced in adolescence. The first evidence that life can, all of a sudden, change for the better. Going from waist-long hair to a pixie cut feels like an apt way to shed my dolorous past, begin again and become somebody else. If I'm honest, I am also engaged in an act of provocation. I'm conscious that I'm inconspicuous. A bad dresser, a bit spooked-looking thanks to the current trend for plucking out all but seven eyebrow hairs. I'm five feet tall, as yet ignorant about the transformative power of make-up and fashion to augment social status,

and it doesn't much help that I'm generally unremit-
tingly insufferable.

I have a battered copy of *Wuthering Heights* in my
bag that I *will* tell you I've read more than once if you
ask me about it. I also have a plethora of completely
untested and thereby absolutely infallible theories about
how people, and the world, work. There was a very
smug man who lived on my street growing up, about
whom my mother would sometimes say 'he'd give your
arse a headache'. He was the sort who insulated himself
against the utter normality of his life by ensuring that
everyone knew how informative and universally relevant
he was, with the rather predictable result of being
incredibly tedious to talk to. You'd leave an exchange
with him feeling mildly concerned that the conversation
had somehow poisoned you. I, too, was that guy.

At sixteen, with all my hair gone and so much weight
quite literally lifted from my shoulders, I have internalised the feminism of my era, which might be both
accurately and pejoratively referred to as 'lipstick
feminism', a popular distillation of ideas that emerged
from feminism's third wave. It was the feminism that
brought femininity back into the fold, launching forth
a generation of girls and women like me, who championed 'feminine' interests and pursuits – beauty being
one – along with other elements of mainstream
feminism which characterised the first two waves.

In her 1792 work *A Vindication of the Rights of Woman*
(which I've also got a copy of in my bag – it's dog-eared

and everything, in case you want proof that I've read every word in there), Mary Wollstonecraft argued that her era's dominant doctrine was based on a confusion. It was not that women were uneducated because they were naturally incapable (a common belief among male thought leaders who kept very astutely observing that women seemed a bit dim in a world where, unrelatedly, they were not permitted to challenge themselves intellectually or leave the house unattended). According to Wollstonecraft, who was not dim, it was that women had become incapable as a result of being denied the education and legal freedoms enjoyed by men. Captured by this rational argument, first-wave feminists focused on obtaining access to education, the vote and legal rights in order to enable women to advocate for themselves in the most fundamental ways. From these basic rights, they argued, others would naturally flow.

The second wave, between the 1960s and 1980s, extended beyond suffrage to consider the way in which female biology was weaponised both legally and socially to limit women's agency. Concepts like bodily autonomy, patriarchy, reproductive rights, violence against women and sexual objectification, as well as fundamental questions of female autonomy and women's identity, came under the feminist umbrella as the movement shifted from a focus on legislative barriers to encompass social and cultural freedoms.

Feminism's third wave, which took place between the 1990s and early to mid-2000s, extended the priorities and critique of second-wave scholars and activists further. It reoriented the focus of the movement to the dual concerns of individual choice and collective identity, embracing intersectionality and the idea of diverse feminist choices. While second-wave feminism, for example, was relatively unified in the idea that sex work is misogynistic exploitation, third-wave ideas began to take a diversified approach, leading to the conclusion that numerous kinds of choices and lives could be feminist. Second-wave feminism had policed women's behaviour to a greater degree, with some feminists designating certain choices as liberated and feminist (like cutting all your hair off) and others, like sex work or choosing to be a stay-at-home mother rather than pursuing a career and financial independence, as invalid or inferior choices indicative of patriarchal subjugation.

The third wave moved to reclaim conceptions of femininity, which had been dismissed as largely oppressive and inferior. Suddenly, wearing make-up, for example, could be either feminist or not, depending on the view of the woman wearing it. In 2001 the film *Legally Blonde* was released, in which Reese Witherspoon plays Elle Woods – the archetypal lipstick feminist. Woods encompasses a plethora of traits loathed by second-wave feminists – she dresses almost exclusively in pink, applies to Harvard Law in a bikini-clad admission video essay exclusively to get her old-money boyfriend back in the hope of marrying him, and loves shopping and beauty treatments.

But Woods is a third-wave feminist heroine, so she stays beautiful by common standards (though her style notably gets a touch more sophisticated and less bubble-gum Barbie) and achieves elevated status in a male-dominated environment. She graduates from Harvard with honours, delivering her cohort's commencement speech. Her new (better, more enlightened) boyfriend observes her elevated value and promptly proposes to her. She can be and has 'it all'. Lipstick feminism was, after all, the feminism which fully internalised the idea that this was possible. That two or more seemingly opposed choices might actually make for a harmonious, fulfilled and actualised life rather than generating a contradiction that leaves women perpetually trying to juggle conflicting priorities. This is the feminism into which I emerged, hairless and full of faux-confidence, and which characterised my formative years.

While I had a sense of the powerful intersection of beauty and feminism back then, I could never have anticipated a version of myself waiting on a phone call in that cupboard fifteen years later, working deep in the heart of media in a culture rooted in a feminism that had lost all meaning. That I would move from the vague sense that there was a transformative and elevating social power in augmenting one's appearance to meet beauty standards to moving around the very top of that female-dominated industry and seeing, in real time, how the sausage is made.

I love beauty. Now that I'm no longer a beauty editor, I've returned to spending all my disposable income on skincare, shampoo (because the next one might be *the one*) and make-up. These things give me profound joy and I've built up years of expertise in them and the real power they possess. Beauty in itself is not the problem. What we don't focus much on, in the public and media conversation around the pressure women feel to look a certain way, is what they are *missing out* on by inhabiting a space in which their physical appearance is not maximised to signal whatever might be most advantageous to them (this quickly comes to equate to what is beautiful to us). This accounts to some degree for the fact that so many women in fashion and beauty media may champion opting out, paring back or investing less but rarely elect to follow this advice themselves. Because beauty is not looking beautiful in some limited, appealing-to-men swimwear model sense. It is proximity to status, money, aspiration, health. It is a reflection of the things that women, who are the world's primary consumers, value. This is of course all largely an illusion but it is a suite of presumptions upon which our culture complacently sits. It is the value of beauty, and the promise of the industry each time we go to buy a new lipstick or to have a beauty treatment. It isn't about reality. It's about appearance.

To court beauty is to be pleasing to have around (we are sadly nicer to and more inclined towards interest in strangers when we consider them to be visually appealing – this is true of women as well as men). To maximise your appearance is to appear to know how the world works and therefore, sadly, to be taken more seriously within it. To do it while signalling minimal effort is to win the game outright. To meet the standard without appearing to try. That impossible bar. This is what gives rise to the aesthetic of top beauty editors in places like Paris and London – minimal make-up that could just be flawless skin, impeccable grooming, soft, healthy hair that glimmers. Understated but high-quality designer clothing and accessories. A general and unmistakable but never obnoxiously overt aura of money.

We can opt out of this beauty hierarchy, but this too signals something. We can tell others to opt out but continue to opt in ourselves. There is no escape from the game but this is only one articulation of the degree to which feminism has become a less definitive and valuable concept. All of this is not a symptom of patriarchy but of feminism itself. My moment of desperate clarity in the cupboard was not a realisation that patriarchy had backed me in here with last year's receipts and the free samples of foot cream and a cake sent over earlier by the people from some designer brand or other. There was no way I could think of to write up this celebrity interview in a form that I could stand over while maintaining my self-respect in this situation, but that wasn't the realisation either.

It was the sudden, unavoidable, destructive awareness that if my editor who expected me to write about a celebrity's weight issues and age believes she's a feminist, and the celebrity selling beauty products while concealing her age believes she's a feminist, and my colleague who keeps asking when my boyfriend is going to propose believes she's a feminist, and my friend who saw that *Cosmopolitan* cover featuring plus-size model Tess Holliday and raved about it but just became vegan to lose weight is a feminist, and my beauty editor friends believe they are feminists, and so do my environment-alist friends who won't stop talking about packaging and waste in the beauty industry, and so are the women I know who champion all women's choices but sneer a little at women who don't have a career, then at worst, feminism has ceased to be a meaningful concept and at best we're going to struggle to figure out what, precisely, feminism actually is.

As far as I could tell, the only thing all of these women have in common is the fact that they are women. Of course feminism's fourth wave, in which we still are and which gained its zenith around the mid-2010s, murmuring in the public consciousness when I was doing this celebrity interview, raised a new problem that somewhat challenges that last common characteristic. The fourth wave is harder to delineate than its predecessors (this is always the case with some-thing that is a live entity) but features at its centre a ferocious debate about what a woman actually is. As a mature concept with a long contextual history, feminism has shifted and morphed over time, and it has been subject to schism, with factions disagreeing on basic concepts.

Yet it's a major problem for a social and political movement that needs cohesion to identify what needs to change and then pursue that change with any success. How can any group get anything done, or achieve clarity, under a feminist banner when there is such internal confusion about what it is to be a feminist? Those who police entry to the club tend to behave – particularly online – as though the criteria are clear and obvious, but the gentlest nudge shows this isn't the case.

Each wave expanded the margins of what it meant to be a feminist and often set people who abided by one era's definition against those who cleaved to another's. There was a time when feminism considered the miniskirt a form of female liberation, but sex work exploitative and antifeminist. It is now more commonly believed (under the banner of feminism, at least) that feminism entails the belief that choices made by individual women are feminist by default. That it is paternalistic to presume that a woman who sells sexual access to her body or has determined that she feels less degraded by posing nude on OnlyFans than she felt by doing low-income service jobs is not able to freely make that determination but only holds this belief because she is a gormless pawn of patriarchy suffering from internalised misogyny.

When I speak with women and ask them what feminism means to them, they tend to give me wildly varied definitions. Even the fluffiest definition, which will usually be something along the lines of 'feminism is just . . .' (watch out for 'justs' – something reductive generally follows) '. . . feminism is just championing women!' is a deeply inadequate and feeble idea, so generalised as to be entirely without substance. Championing women for what – their choices? If so, which choices? Does my choice to cut off all my hair at sixteen count? What about my choice to get married and buy an engagement ring, or my choice to eat two consecutive bags of Marks & Spencer Cheese Tasters in bed while watching *Dune* last Christmas? To write unequivocally in favour of abortion access but also write compassionately about why pro-life people may not agree with that position? To write up the turgid cupboard interview with the celebrity? Are those all feminist choices? Feminism is about choice, and yet the subtext obviously values some choices above others.

A belief system, an ideology must be built on the basis of foundational principles and ideas – something around which people can coalesce and advocate for change. Without this, we have factions with varying levels of adherence to conflicting principles all claiming authority over the one true interpretation. We have second-wave feminists shouting at third-wavers about motherhood, lipstick and sex work while fourth-wavers run in screaming to argue with the other two about who the movement should be representing. These are all interesting debates in their own way, but they cannot ever make progress in the context of a meaningful coalition and it does not help that each faction seems to point to the others and confidently declare them not just wrong but deluded and possibly also evil. Once there is fundamental disagreement about the most basic concepts upon which a movement is based as well as who it is actually advocating for, it has become (pragmatically speaking) useless.

I thought about the trajectory of my own identification with feminism from observing the gender disparities around me growing up to the feminism of my twenties and beyond. At that time, my major focus mirrored that of many women around me – campaigning and advocating for abortion access for Irish women, who were prevented from terminating unwanted or medically unsafe pregnancies by the eighth amendment to Ireland's constitution. The country's history is littered with horror stories of young women dying in childbirth, becoming pregnant as a result of rape, and bleeding on flights back from the UK, where they were forced to travel to access abortion services, if they had the means. It is a macabre history of state and Church interference in the autonomy of the individual. All of this arose within the context of a deeply, formally and systemically sexist past. Married women were not permitted to work in the civil service until 1973. Contraception was not widely available until the early nineties and divorce was not legalised until 1996. When the referendum to repeal the eighth amendment passed in 2018, I considered the last major legal barrier to women's agency in my home country to have been lifted. We hadn't reached post-feminist utopia, but it seemed to me that the last basic freedom was no longer inaccessible to us.

When I moved to the UK soon after the referendum and found myself sitting in that cupboard after the phone call with the famous woman, I considered the definition this person, associated in her youth with a feminist shift in popular culture, shared when I asked her what feminism means to her now. Be kind, she suggested. It all *just* comes down to that. Feminism is about women being kind to one another. I had conducted at least three other interviews in the last year in which a female celebrity had given me this line and had started to wonder if there were publicists advising them to say this as a means of keeping out of the fractious public discourse on feminism and gender. I felt something like despair but also recognised a dark logic in how someone who has major cultural influence among women might come to give such a vague and flaccid definition as this.

To suggest that a complex and contested set of ideas is simple and clear as long as we merely reduce the entire concept to whatever the speaker feels most comfortable with themselves (or whatever sells a product) is to ignore a major problem for women. I sat quietly in the cupboard and had two realisations in quick succession. One was that, much as I love beauty, I didn't want working in magazines to be my primary job any more. I needed to begin carving out an escape route (that would take four years, mostly due to a pandemic and cowardice, not necessarily in that order). The second was that I was no longer a feminist. Not because I think women are less valuable than men. Not because I'm aggressively in favour of intra-female unkindness or because I don't 'champion women' (though I don't, because that phrase is a vortex of virtue-signalling frippery). I was no longer a feminist because by using the word to describe myself I might be understood to be declaring any one or a combination of a thousand often opposing fealties, and consequently it had no meaning.

Feminism has become a derelict house. I have no idea what it means to be a feminist, and neither do you. Find, if you can, the golden thread that runs through it from Wollstonecraft to the current day. You might argue that it's power. The maximisation, defence or establishing of women's power to act according to their own choice and to be recognised as agents within society – not merely people who are acted upon – legislatively, socially, biologically. You might say that feminism is a movement that seeks to establish and defend the right of women to both 'do' and to 'have'. You might argue that it's being kind. I wouldn't, because that's so depressing. The term has become a monument to other eras but a decayed representation of all of them. If it can refer to everything, then it doesn't refer to anything. We need new words, or new ideas. Ideally both.

There is something comforting in this, though. The incident in the cupboard was the beginning of a route to realisation. Like so many of the women around me, I had been figuratively hunched over with a general sense of widely branching and deeply rooted failure. A sense that I was trying very hard indeed but never quite meeting the standards I was imposing on myself. In relationships, family or career. During my life in London and since, there were two major themes that seemed to present significant challenges and invite constant commentary from the world around me. I wasn't married, and I didn't have children. Both of these purportedly celebration-worthy feminist choices resulted in constant questions and unsolicited criticism, especially the choice not to have children.

I did get married, in the end. I had grown utterly weary of the pitying looks and probing questions from women I knew. The contrast between the values they claimed to live by as modern women and the obsession with weddings – how much a man should spend on a ring and the appetite for a huge event that centres the woman as though a wedding is the greatest achievement of her life – was too glaring. The details of the traditional proposal, when a man is supposed to come to a woman on his knee(s), in worship and supplication, begging her to end his suffering with a gift that cost at least three months' salary (apparently), made me more than a little uncomfortable. Like so many, it is an archaism that we senselessly keep while discarding other, less personally advantageous ones. That too is fine, but only if we are honest with ourselves about what we really value.

Are we equals, or are we not? If, on average, men have their cake and eat it by forgoing marriage (as my probing questioners constantly suggested seven years into a relationship), it seems that women do the same in the process from proposal to wedding. The whole thing announces, 'I am a treasure, a gift, an ornament made valuable through this man's choice. Come to the wedding and celebrate us, sure, but mostly, celebrate *me*.'

Yes, we can subvert the tropes that were at some point rooted in religious tradition – the woman can propose to the man, or the people being married can have different genders or, none, or, like J. and me, you can make something of a joke of the whole thing by not really doing it 'properly'. You can't escape, though. Within our culture and at its root, marriage has philosophical underpinnings and religious origins which still dictate what it means and, to a large extent, what it looks like. These ideas continue to determine why we desire it and what we are trying to declare to the world by getting married. You might be trying to say, 'I'd like this guy to be the person who decides when to pull the plug if I get hit by a bus,' but you're also unavoidably responding to cultural pressures to say,

'This is a meaningful, committed relationship, and we are respectable people.'

The wedding itself was not really a wedding. Or not, as my mother would have said, 'so's you'd know it.' We eloped in 2020, a week before the first lockdown, and sort of piggy-backed on the virus as an excuse to not quite have a wedding. Or not so's you'd know it. It was the two of us at the pretty but somehow still clinical town hall in Twickenham, a leafy suburb in affluent south-west London, with two friends as the legally required witnesses and a bloviating registrar whose tired congratulations were the tonal equivalent of a cup of cold tea.

It occurred to me during the ceremony (which consisted of the bored registrar reading from his stained book with intermittent demands that we stand up or sign papers) that this would likely be many people's idea of the worst imaginable wedding. A dreadful, anticlimactic affair, all over in fifteen minutes. Not at all the sort of thing that merits special diets or dress fittings or a reception at a country hotel. With a total attendance of four, that country hotel reception seemed excessive, so instead we walked round the corner – three suits and a cream dress – to a local café and got some breakfast. I had French toast. Then we all went back to work.

There is immense judgement of long-term relationships that show no imminent inclination towards matrimony. I for one got tired of the jabbing queries, always delivered in a tone which suggested that J. was neglectful in not making the commitment and that I had no self-respect in allowing him to shirk it. In heterosexual relationships, we still largely view marriage as a thing that happens to women and is initiated by men. In a traditional religious context, this may be truer (though not always). In secular environments, it seems that the opposite is more usually true. Women are generally the architects but they must generate the conditions which encourage the man to ask. What a grim pressure.

The wedding did not change the relationship, which was the most important of my life before and remains that way. I'm glad of the label in some respects. The legal protection and the financial clarity and the fact that the language of marriage has put an end to the probing questions I faced – J. unsurprisingly got far fewer of them. I'm glad that if that bus does ever come for me and the plug needs to be pulled, the choice will go to someone I trust to do what is best for me (if you're reading this, pull the damn plug). It says a lot about us as a culture, though, that we believe a commitment we make of our own volition is less meaningful than one rubber-stamped by the state, represented by the blustering, indifferent registrar with the crooked tie. Haven't we learned by now that nothing we do is made truly meaningful by general consensus?

If I'm honest, though, I was happy before, and the way that we got married, while it was just what we wanted, registered with those around me as a failure regardless of the fact that it was done in part to appease them. Some magazine editors have since commissioned me to write about the elopement as part of a trend which is characterised by an interesting departure from tradition (read: feminist choice) but most of the people physically present in my life did not see it that way. My mother-in-law wailed over the phone as though she'd been shot (lockdown fell right after the wedding) and felt that we had selfishly robbed her of an experience that she should have been part of. One of my friends asked, one hand on my knee as though she was condoling with me after a bereavement, if I felt short-changed by the lack of a 'big day'. I was irritated by the implication that the wedding I had chosen somehow happened *to* me, like getting spattered with seagull faeces when you're trying to enjoy a nice ice cream at the beach.

So many women I worked with looked crestfallen or baffled when they noticed the wedding band and asked me about the wedding. We married in part to shut people up (was that a feminist choice? I'm guessing not), because I could no longer bear the constant questions and, of course, it didn't actually solve the problem. We hadn't yet decided whether we wanted to be parents (presuming we had the capacity to be) and as someone raised by a single mother, I craved the sense of security and legal clarity that marriage would theoretically provide. I say theoretically as my parents were married and theoretical support was really the only type my father provided to my mother while she raised us alone. All the pressures pointed to marriage. We got married. Within a few months of eloping, the baby questions started coming. Four years later, they're still coming.

For a long time, I simply did not make up my mind about motherhood. That in itself will evoke judgement but my indecision was not based in ignorance. Women are aware of the biological window closing. For women living within the baffling, contradictory vortex of modern feminist culture at least, which is to say women who absorb mainstream cultural outputs in the UK, Ireland or the US, that awareness creeps in around your late twenties. It lingers for the decade to follow and often beyond, room for flexibility and vacillation narrowing as the window slowly closes. If you somehow were not aware of your own biological limitations, people tell you very directly, as though you haven't noticed that your back now sometimes hurts in the morning for no reason. The window looms above like a bell jar or a gyre of angry vultures scenting a womb on the turn. Sometimes people – interestingly, almost always women who are older than I am – ask me whether I'm aware that I don't have forever to have a baby. To these women I say this: 'We've just met, and this is a dinner party. I'm unbelievably uncomfortable right now. Could you just pass the salad, please?'

In its mainstream media representation, feminism is obsessed by the motherhood label. Caught within a pendulously indecisive discourse that generates conflict between the life-altering, elevated, cosmic-love conception of motherhood as the most meaningful and challenging role in a woman's life and the choice to opt out of what has so long been seen as every woman's biological destiny to pursue a different kind of life. Of course, into the gap between the two fall both the mothers who feel unhappy and unfulfilled within their role – a position still so taboo that it is rarely openly discussed or acknowledged – and the women who long to be mothers but cannot, for whatever reason. Those women face the same tedious judgement as those who, like me, simply decide not to have children. There is a deep cruelty in that – it is surely easier to be judged harshly for a decision you have actively embraced than one you haven't.

Although in a world where we are consistently told that women's choices are valid and the exercising of choice is in itself a wonderful articulation of the feminism that unites us all, the pressure to have children is astoundingly prolonged and palpable. Motherhood is often treated as a sort of reductive, retro label and yet, for so many women for extended periods of life, motherhood *is* their orienting label and mode of identity. In a period and role of overwhelming change and demand, mothers can be left feeling that they are somehow failing by becoming, for a time, restricted to this one label, though we live in a world which both normatively and financially leaves them with no breathing room at all. No matter where you're standing as a woman, you are told your choice should be celebrated and yet, the moment you make it, that choice is weighed against popular feminist conceptions of what a self-actualised woman should look like, and it turns out none of us are doing it right.

The dissonance that so many women feel and carry in their minds represents the dissonance that exists within feminism as an identity. It all feels a bit off because it *is* off. All established concepts have history – baggage – and the more they have, the more generally competing interpretations of the concept will emerge over time. That is where we are with feminism. Wildly varied permutations of it have developed since its first-wave genesis, and not all share the same foundational principles. Both means and ends differ depending on the version of feminism a person identifies with. It is no longer a schism in feminism but a rupture, and every fragment claims it's the one true answer and the only way to be a woman in the world. Every faction tells women a competing story of who and what they are, and how they should be living.

As things currently stand, this is why – if you're a woman – you probably feel like you can't get anything right. Not necessarily because you're falling short but because you live under a feminist banner that endlessly holds you to two opposing standards at once, not in the name of patriarchy, as has often traditionally been claimed and has historically been the case, but in the name of feminism itself.

49

You should be hard, but you should also be nurturing. You should aspire to a traditional, monogamous marriage, but you should also forgo archaic traditions and rituals. You should be entirely self-directed, but also defer to others and conform to perceptions of appropriate ideas and behaviour. You should put yourself first as a form of radical self-actualisation, but choosing not to have children is selfish so you should have them. If you do, you should be with them all the time but remember to take time for yourself. You should celebrate traditional forms of femininity but also desire to see women excel in traditionally male domains. Capitalism is inherently bad and devalues individuals but if you don't exchange labour for money, your agency and value as a woman are reduced. So be a devoted mother but don't be wedded to your job, but excel at work or you're setting women back as a group. Alright? You should also be inclusive of forms of gender non-expression and gender non-solidarity, as well as forms of gender solidarity and gender conformity. But don't be overly partial in any one direction. If you have no idea what any of that means, don't say so out loud. Just smile and nod.

It's clear enough that some of these beliefs are very much mutually exclusive. They cannot all coexist within a sane mind – or in the confines of one cupboard or be represented by one haircut – at once. No woman can 'do' all of these to the satisfaction of the dominant doctrine. Not because she is failing, but because the doctrine is confused and fraying to pieces before our eyes. These beliefs, parcelled together, amount to no maxim and no mandate. They are, like feminism within popular culture at present, a confused mess.

And to the people who got this far and still find themselves muttering, narrow-eyed and confident, 'She'd change her mind if she had a baby,' I could say, 'Be kind,' but I know from experience what a wet lettuce of a phrase that is. So instead, I'll say the following in a tone of deep weariness:

Just pass the salad, please.

2

Mad

I felt wise and cynical as all hell.
— Sylvia Plath, *The Bell Jar*

THERE IS SOMETHING ABOUT intense emotions – namely our own – that we implicitly trust. We usually don't have sound cause to trust them apart from the fact that the stronger the feeling, the more objective it appears to us. It was this strange power, the source of so much that is both wonderful and deeply stupid about human beings, which led me to study emotions and the philosophy of psychology. It was the hope that thinking carefully enough about emotions might help me to understand why we are the way we are. Why it is that we can both create exquisite art and behave like strange angry babies on social media. How we came to be a species capable of both appreciating the work of Shakespeare and getting into a verbal altercation with our adult sibling over a game of Monopoly that didn't go our way on a Wednesday evening.

I hoped that studying how philosophers and psychologists have thought about emotions might help me to develop more control over my own. That was probably a bad call. When I was considering studying psychology and philosophy at university I read the prospectus for the undergraduate psychology degree at Trinity College in Dublin. It contained a caveat amounting to something along the lines of the following: studying psychology is not the best option for people with a history of psychological issues. Not yet realising that everyone has psychological issues, I took the warning to heart and decided to study philosophy and English literature instead. The latter is a discipline which has produced some of the most unhinged ideas in the history of human thought. It was not a thing to study if you were aiming to become saner. Regardless, my interest in emotions remained long after I left behind the study of English. In literature, I had been looking to make sense of the world and to distinguish what was emotion from what wasn't. This too was a mistake. We aren't beings of reason *or* emotion, but both. As in so many other ways, we evade straightforward classification. We have no way of interpreting our experiences without filtering them through feeling.

When I was growing up, everything was emotional turmoil. My parents flung their weaponised feelings (or approximations of them, cloaked as facts about the other person) over the furniture at one another. Emotions, dense and barbed, forested our lives, their

54

sprawling foliage impeding any clear view of the present, past or future.

The truth seemed clear to every person around me but differed fundamentally depending on who you asked. If there was a fact of the matter, it seemed as elusive as the precise source of a bleed when an artery has been nicked. Swamped. Indeterminate. Just another red thing in a red landscape. Feeling and reality – such as we might understand it – were presented always askance, like revelation from the experience of its viewer, and described as truer than the same paltry presentation made by anyone else. Things were as true as they felt.

There were the emotions expressed, and the ones truly experienced, and the bedrock or unspoken but foundational beliefs from which they emerged. Vortex. Vortex. Everything was ruction and undulating ground. You could never get a foothold. There was nothing but relative truth and that truth was relative to whoever was loudest, whoever was paying the bills, whoever was sober, whoever was most invested in portraying themselves as the victim. The truth was a slick fish. A length of alien muscle too quick to grasp. Anxiety, fear, uncertainty became normality.

Stories about how the world works emerged from the patterns I observed around me. People were fickle and could not be relied upon. Relationships were not intimate and meaningful unless they involved emotional chaos and pain. People will say one thing but they may mean and do another entirely. When confronted with this, they won't recognise this account as describing their actions. They will feel wronged, and so will you, and it will become impossible to determine what actually happened, whose harm is false. Consequently, the world was a place to fear. One in which I needed to be canny, guarded and supremely cautious to compensate for the understanding and experience I lacked. Unsurprisingly, I ventured into this world as I had conceived of it, reluctantly, certain that I would be hurt and that I was incapable of preventing this. This was the only version of the world I was equipped to see. The outcomes I feared were the only ones I knew how to contribute to. The patterns written into me through limited experience played themselves out. Anger logically followed and built into something else.

Inside the confines of my own mind, even these days, I am not at all decent to myself. I'm not sure that any of us are gentle to ourselves there, where the very worst and weakest aspects of us dominate as we watch with the weariness of total predictability or, occasionally, the horror of shocked disgust. Few of us would want anyone else to witness the unfettered contents of our internal monologue. I conduct conversations internally which, if engaged in with a partner (who is supposed to have my welfare at least vaguely in mind), would prompt any loyal friend to advise me to leave that piece of shit as soon as I can hurl my stuff into a suitcase and change my number. 'How can you let anyone talk to you like that?' becomes a more complex question when you are the person ... talking to you like that.

Occasionally, I will respond to these verbal assaults aloud, saying something along the lines of 'No! You absolute fucking *wank gasket.*' I am at the kitchen sink, a thin foam of washing-up liquid effervescing against the downy hairs on my forearms like a visceral fear response from deep in my DNA, holding a novelty mug from an Easter egg I've had since Easter eggs came in novelty mugs, and I am shouting aloud at myself. If any unfortunate person (say, one I'm married to) happened to amble past and bear witness to these tense exchanges, I would not blame them if their face transformed into a collection of shapes universally understood as conveying horrified concern. This is the face we arrange and present to a mad person. I get that. I know it. I've had plenty of cause to arrange that particular face myself.

A lot of people might say – with wry fondness or exasperated exaggeration – that their family is a bit mad. A touch strange. Often, what they mean by this is that they once discovered their mother smoking at the back of the garden and realised that she's been successfully concealing the habit from them for twenty years. *Who is she? Who is this woman?* they'll wonder, kind of horrified but maybe also slightly grudgingly impressed. Or that the table is awkwardly silenced as grandpa makes weird, bigoted statements between requests to pass the gravy at Sunday lunch ('Everyone knows that the Welsh would invade North Korea tomorrow if they had the ships. Sure they love coal.') Or their dad pulls out an exhausted-looking ukulele at family parties and plays 'Born in the USA' while everyone under fifty visibly shrinks into themselves. Oh, he's on a chair now. He's doing a ukulele solo like he has his whole youth to relive and his own dead father to prove wrong, and part of you leaves your body while the rest of you envies his positively ablative confidence. You wonder if other people's dads are like this but you presume not. How could they be? The *Daily Mail* would never stop writing about it.

This is the sort of thing people mean when they discuss their odd family. They don't generally mean literal madness of the old-fashioned, dissociative 'my doctors are trying to murder me and the government has taken all my blood and replaced it with liquefied microchips in the night' sort. The type where people live in a reality that so clearly isn't the one shared by the rest of us that they are sectioned and hospitalised for their own safety, or the kind where a person's natural instinct to live is so subverted by self-loathing and substance abuse that they take bizarre risks that put their children directly in danger. The kind of madness, in short, where the wheels fall off and the rules no longer apply. The kind where you watch someone reject any consensus view of the world in which they live, gather their hospital gown up around their knees and jump out the Overton window.

In my early teens, I was visiting a friend's house when she received the news of her father's premature death from a heart attack. Her heartbreak and devastation are embossed on my memory. It was as though everything solid in the world dissolved around her the moment she was told he was gone. Part of me marvelled at the pain she so clearly experienced, thinking, *Is this what it is to have a father who loves you and to lose him?* I considered that this man's heart had to stop to justify his absence from her life. He had been kind, present, reliable. It was cruel. It was unfair but it was a respectable form of non-consensual valediction. Blameless. Causally uncomplicated, if unrelentingly dreadful. A true and clear loss.

When people at school asked me where my father was, I would reply expressionlessly that he was off somewhere pursuing his passion for beverages. It was not the whole story but it also wasn't strictly incorrect. I was fourteen. 'Where is he, though?' they'd insist, as though further probing could solve the mystery. I'd look at them like a cynical old woman exhausted by the company of exuberant children. I could only marvel at the idea that they'd expect me to know the answer to such a question. How could I know where he was if he didn't bother to tell me?

I come from a long line of addicts, malcontents, maladjusts (you have to create the right words to describe what you see as the need arises) and loons. You don't emerge from that without shouting at yourself occasionally. There's plenty to shout about. In fact, if you have a weird enough upbringing, audibly calling yourself a *wank gasket* at the kitchen sink is really a perfectly rational thing to do. When you are raised in unhealthy and aberrant conditions, you learn behaviours that serve and preserve you in those environments but may have the less helpful effect of making your life in the wider world more difficult.

There are things you do not know how to do as most others do them, like socialising with people your age, navigating new environments without intense anxiety and a haunting sense of being a fraud on the cusp of discovery, or distinguishing constructive criticism from total evisceration of your value and right to be in the room.

In childhood and young adulthood, all of these were problems I consistently failed to manage. A description that was frequently applied to me was 'sensitive'. Whether the word was used as an insult ('don't be so ... / 'you're just too ...') or as an excuse or compliment to justify or validate my emotional reactions ('You're a very ...'), it was a story I was told about myself until I absorbed it as a fact. Both a terminal weakness and a badge of ego. It wasn't that I was less robust than some other people my age or that my coping skills were less well developed. It was that I was more attuned than they were. I was smarter than they were, more highly connected to the sadness and injustice in the world. I ignored the clear evidence of pain and struggle around all me and elevated my own to a gift and a curse. A second sight. *I get it*, I thought. *And they don't.* This is who I am. I'm short. I like reading. I'm sensitive. Facts.

Perhaps you've been labelled with that word or hitched it around someone in your life. Maybe, as I did, you shelter behind it. Maybe you've bent it around you like a shield. The category Highly Sensitive Person (HSP) isn't a medical or diagnostic term, but one of those apparently appealing socially descriptive labels with which people tend to self-diagnose or self-identify after seeing a few minutes of barely coherent TikTok content on the subject. The term resonates with people who can find things difficult. People who have struggled to emerge from challenging situations or the insensitivity of other people without feeling damaged in a way that others consider disproportionate to the injury. People like me.

The phrase was coined by psychologist Elaine Aron in 1996 and refers to individuals who display increased emotional sensitivity and stronger-than-standard reactions to internal and external stimuli like pain or noise, as well as a tendency to become overwhelmed, anxious or depressed as a result. Importantly, this isn't a medically recognised feature of neurodivergence or a condition, but a behavioural descriptor gesturing with convenient vagueness toward a type of personality. While the descriptor appears to have become popular among women in particular, psychologists tend not to like it all that much, mostly because it's largely unsubstantiated within the psychology literature. Aron hypothesised that 15–20 per cent of the population qualifies as an HSP. It isn't particularly surprising that it is a far less popular self-description among men, undermining as it does traditional ideals around masculinity and how a man interacts with – and is permitted to be emotionally impacted by – the world.

Whether we have 'innate' traits at all is very much a conversation rather than a settled question, but high sensitivity seems more like a confluence of traits than a trait in itself. Even if being 'highly sensitive' did refer to a group of traits within one individual, there's nothing to suggest these traits are not learned. That which can be learned can be augmented or overwritten with new information and habits. If it exists – and I don't believe it does in any meaningful sense – the HSP is not fixed. This is so often the problem with descriptive labels: they are very quickly adopted by people who view them as prescriptive and then, in one act of self-serving sophistry or misunderstanding, *how we behave* becomes both *who we are* and delineates the boundary of our potential to be anything else, so that to suggest that the label may not serve a person is to attack their very identity.

Up until my mid-to-late twenties, every experience seemed to seep in as though I were utterly permeable. I was easily overwhelmed by crowds, loud noise or sudden changes of plan. I was thrown easily, and consequently, thrown often. I found being alive generally deeply hurtful and difficult, and from the age of fourteen struggled dreadfully with what was later called depression. At the time I just considered it old-fashioned misery. It became so bad that by my early twenties, I didn't want to be alive any more. Everything went dark, and when I felt least able and least inclined, I finally had to learn the skills I had been drowning without. I did a *lot* of cognitive behavioural therapy and began to create new stories to live by. Better and more constructive ones. I learned to do things that frightened me, to connect with other people, and to fail without feeling like it made my efforts futile. I learned that comfort and safety are not the same thing despite the fact that we frequently conflate them.

I *was* sensitive, but this was not some neurological destiny written into generations of broken brains giving rise to my own. It was not a gift making me deep and poetic and more capable of meaningful feeling than other people (what a megalomaniacal 'main character' theory that is). I was being kind of a *wank gasket* – self-involved, more attached to my own immediate comfort than my ability to improve by challenging myself slowly over time, and unwilling to get out of my own way when there was plenty in my way already. Reluctant to consider that there were ways to exist in the world that didn't model the one I grew up in. Labels may help describe how you have been up to now, but that's all. You are not doomed, predestined or done. I had not realised that. Not really.

I fought what I saw as my fate but never quite shook the sense that it would get me in the end. For a long time, that belief shaped my response to challenges that rose up to meet me and, in so doing, predetermined the outcome.

*

Without personal agency, there is no hope. We have to take responsibility for ourselves in order to improve our situation and outcomes. The fewer caring people we have around us, the more essential this becomes – tragically, it is those without a support network who sink fastest and suffer most acutely. Without a sense of ownership over our own well-being, we are doomed. So we have to help ourselves. This is true of those suffering with mental illness insofar as they have the presence of mind and the resources to do it (of course, not everyone does – a person in psychosis does not know they are ill). However, if we truly believe ourselves incapable of change, then we are – we create that outcome. Still, there are limits. I cannot 'believe' myself to the top of Mount Everest without money, expertise, prolonged training and the right equipment. I cannot 'believe' myself into feeling safe or free if I'm locked in a cage full of tigers with no access to the key. There are elements we can control. Others, we can't.

In the UK, young people are clearly struggling. In a 2017 NHS survey of children and young people's mental health, 10.1 per cent of people in the 17–19 age category were found to have a probable mental disorder. In 2022 the number had risen to 25.7 per cent. While the pandemic affected mental health as detrimentally as it affected just about everything else, that is alarming nonetheless. The NHS Annual IAPT (Improving Access to Psychological Therapy) report for 2021–2 states that 1.81 million people were referred to IAPT in that time; and 1.24 million entered a course of treatment. Waiting times to access these forms of generally short-term talk therapy can be extensive.

Some people drop out while waiting. Many become more ill – some develop much more serious symptoms and thus more acute needs in the interim. Some don't have the emotional or financial resources to be able to handle the wait. Some access the treatment and realise that mental health problems don't arise in a vacuum. There is strong correlation between poverty and mental illness. It is challenging to establish definitive causal patterns – I think it works both ways, that being poor (with all its attendant stresses, insecurities and exposure to wider social problems) contributes to mental ill health, while mental ill health (with its tendency to interrupt a person's ability to function as well as maintain their health and safety) makes people poorer. It's a vicious cycle.

According to the Mental Health Foundation, children and adults living in the lowest 20 per cent income bracket in Britain are two to three times more likely to develop mental health problems than those in the highest income bracket. The lower your access to support and resources, the higher the chance that your issues will spiral into severity before you are considered entitled to help when you cannot pay for it privately.

The lower your access to support and resources, the less likely it is that you will have someone in your life who is themselves in a position to recognise that you need help, step in and successfully advocate for you inside an inefficient and chronically overburdened mental healthcare system. Without these things, there's a higher likelihood that you will seek out available substances in order to self-medicate and alleviate your suffering. Of course you will – it might be what feels like the only means of feeling better or meeting the demands of basic function when you have nobody else to help you.

Access to high-quality, consistent mental healthcare can be hard to come by even if you have the resources to pay for it. It is, like all others, an industry which is most lucrative when meeting the needs of people who can pay the most. Not everyone is a candidate for therapy, and not everyone needs it. Our culture is generally becoming increasingly therapised. You can't throw an iced matcha latte in London's wealthier suburbs without hitting someone uttering words and phrases like 'boundaries', 'emotional space', 'self-care', 'mental resources' and 'honouring my needs'. I enjoy the profligate indulgence of an iced latte (minus the matcha) as much as the next burnt-out, overtherapised millennial writer. However, this kind of language is less often found among the socio-economically disadvantaged, whose needs are not honoured as a matter of course, and whose 'boundaries' are rarely relevant to anyone. No one is 'holding space' for their 'lived experience' and if they react to this reality by behaving in ways that reject conformity or look either loud or aggressive by middle-class standards, there is no compassion for that either.

In a world obsessed with symbolising concern about poor mental health to disguise a total lack of substantial commitment to materially improving it, access to mental healthcare is far more complex than the usual finger-wagging arguments from people who audited an economics seminar that one time. Those for whom 'Capitalism = Bad!' constitutes an entire argument. People are not unable to access public healthcare because private healthcare exists. Personally, I would be more inclined to trust a professional of my choosing to provide mental healthcare than an agent of a socialised healthcare system, which, by its very design, does not and cannot prioritise individual well-being. It must choose whom to treat, how and when based on guidelines that inherently conflict with and are irrelevant to the need of an individual patient who is suffering in the moment – elements like budget, age and the number of adequately trained and available medical professionals. Equal (lack of) access to bad care for all is not necessarily better than some access to adequate care for some. Inequality of care access registers in the gut as an injustice, and the boundary-setting middle-class iced-latte drinkers writing Instagram posts about the latest diagnostic buzzword can enrage people as though their good fortune creates the dearth of access for people who suffer much more severely and need help much more urgently on average.

But it's more complex than that. When faced with what philosophers call 'wicked problems', we are drawn to the lure of a simple solution. Someone to blame. It isn't simple. We're all to blame and that is the ugliness we prefer to avoid. There is often little incentive for governments to prioritise the severely mentally ill – they're not big voters. They have bigger problems and priorities. They can behave strangely, seem frightening, or exhibit what can appear from the outside to be almost breathtaking selfishness. They can be unsympathetic victims and they can harm people around them in real and lasting ways.

No one can shore up their political position by helping the mentally ill, so those most in need are often forgotten and patronised with tokenistic gestures and entreaties to 'talk' about their feelings or feeble slogans. 'It's okay not to be okay' is not a phrase that stems the metaphorical bleed of severe mental distress. In most cases, men are not jumping into rivers – as they do in frightening numbers in my home town of Limerick city, which consistently has the highest suicide rate in

Ireland, where 80 per cent of people who die by suicide are men – because they aren't able to talk about feeling stressed, traumatised, hopeless or upset. It is because they determine that talking cannot solve so vast an array of problems as the one that brought them to the bank or the bridge on a dark night. Talking exposes a problem and that makes for a constructive beginning, but it is nothing like a solution. To talk openly is to render a vulnerable person maximally vulnerable and then ... leave them to go about their business. Encouraging people to talk about how they are feeling is, in so many ways, cheap.

So we're aware that the problem is vast and frightening. A systemic rot that goes many miles deeper than transparent gestures and patronising tokenism. Once you find yourself experiencing a crisis of mental illness, what then? What good is awareness if nothing comes after it? How helpful is knowing you're in trouble – saying you're in trouble and defining the contours of your distress – if help never comes?

We have a delusional habit, no doubt worsened by social media activism, of treating acknowledgement of a problem like doing something about it. It's not. When help is not there or a person is not capable of accessing it, it can be impossible for them – or for anyone who interacts with them – to situate their identity outside a mental health label, which is in part why mental health labels are so complex. Sometimes, for reasons outside their control, some people are trapped. Without the help they need and deserve, they cope as best they can. They might do this in unorthodox or uncon- structive ways. They deserve compassion and they often receive contempt.

I write this because the section that follows is my own story with mental health labels. The adoption and the casting off of just such a label, to be precise. But here is the key factor – I *did* have help. I was incred- ibly lucky. Lucky in a way that saved my life. I helped myself by controlling the things I could control, even when I felt I couldn't or didn't want to. And yet I was able to do this because I was not doing it alone. Some labels are a communal effort to navigate. Sometimes we need people around us to help us see that we are not reducible to one element of our experience. That we are more than a label – not doomed, destined or done. There is rigour and hard work and determina- tion, but some things are also about luck. Sometimes the difference between sanity and madness comes down to nothing more than the presence of a net when you fall.

*

After my diagnosis at eighteen and a more serious depressive episode that followed shortly after, labels felt very important – like a sure route to myself in a heaving, lightless room. A point of clarity, of objectivity, in a relative world. Something true. 'Depression' was one label to which I was particularly attached. A dark seam that crept like a gluey sludge through the turgid arterial network of my family's history. Abuse, neglect, maladjustment, constant stress about money – how could such things leave any legacy but incapacity and despair in every new generation?

That word – that diagnosis – felt like an explanation for everything I couldn't do and also a justification, rather than a description of a set of behaviours and feelings I had learned in response to a particular environment. I worked hard to manage what I saw as an immutable condition through therapy and, for a time, medication, but the way that I thought about the label robbed me of agency – the only means by which I might truly get better – and ultimately impeded my progress.

The diagnosis was also the wellspring from which the questions would later trickle forth. This word, depression, made me rather uninterested in 'my truth', and more interested in the truth, because that condition is a notorious liar. Despite the ways that we flatten and parody it to make it fit the narrow confines of public discourse, depression is not as simple as a dopamine or serotonin deficiency. It cannot be physically tested for, and it is not the same as that infamous broken leg people like to wax lyrical about when trying to explain the validity of depression as a medical condition – 'You wouldn't tell him to walk on a broken leg!' the platitude goes, to clarify that depression entails an incapacity to act rather than an unwillingness.

At nineteen, after years of isolation and a sense of complete desolation and bafflement that stalked me through adolescence, I found myself on a floor. I had left home for the first time after securing a place at Trinity College in Dublin, where I proceeded to flounder both mentally and academically while those around me were seemingly bred for this environment whose norms were entirely alien to me. Eventually, I lay down on the floor of my room in shared student accommodation and couldn't think of a single compelling reason to get up again. I watched dumbly as the hours passed and the ceiling grew dark above me.

My legs might as well have been broken. They didn't feel connected to me. I was adrift somewhere in the periphery of my own body. For some weeks prior, I had sat reading as usual in the library and observed that one day the words simply began moving around the page and didn't stop. They would not stay still long enough for me to capture their meaning; they trickled off the paper and off the screen, denying me access. *Ah*, I thought, my skin prickling with a needling warmth that registered as both terror and familiarity, like a hot flush of shame crimsoning out through my skin. *Here it is then. The insanity that was always inevitable anyway.* The books closed themselves to me. When I couldn't read, I lost my reason to try and my capacity to get up, so I didn't.

Here is how it works when a person is diagnosed with depression; a condition which is, from the outside, nothing more than an immaterial set of inscrutable behavioural characteristics. You visit a psychiatrist. He or she will ask you questions. Based on the answers you provide to those questions, they will determine whether you are clinically depressed.

To do this, they will drag out (literally or figuratively) a copy of the *DSM-5-TR*, the revised fifth edition of the *Diagnostic and Statistical Manual of Mental Disorders*. They will look at the nine listed indicators of depressive disorder. These are things like 'Significant weight loss when not dieting or weight gain ... or decrease or increase in appetite nearly every day.' And 'Diminished ability to think or concentrate, or indecisiveness, nearly every day (either by subjective account or as observed by others).' In order to receive a diagnosis of depression, you must exhibit or identify with five of the nine symptoms on the list. At least one of them must be either 'Depressed mood most of the day, nearly every day, as indicated by either subjective report (e.g., feels sad, empty, hopeless) or observation made by others (e.g., appears tearful). (Note: In children and adolescents, can be irritable mood.)' or 'Markedly diminished interest or pleasure in all, or almost all, activities most of the day, nearly every day (as indicated by either subjective account or observation.)'

Those who are unfamiliar with the process generally imagine something more overtly scientific, something more comfortingly substantial and delineated; a litmus test, or a bright light blasted into the retina – anything that might be quantified. Just recently, a friend of mine who has started a course of antidepressants told me with full conviction that she needs them due to a chemical imbalance in her brain. Her doctor assured her that this was the case, and she feels markedly better now than before she took the drugs. This is a good outcome, but her doctor had no evidence whatsoever that her low mood was caused by a chemical imbalance.

She used the *DSM-5-TR* to diagnose mild depression and gave my friend information about her mental state which is impossible to prove, or even know. Psychiatry is trial and error, and to some extent, an exercise in faith. Drugs are thrown at problems until the right combination of them is found (drugs, not problems), and this can be identified by observable behavioural changes, the improvement of physical symptoms and the reports of the patient. We comfort ourselves with narratives of chemical imbalances, and of course they may be involved in depression, or many cases of it. But the diagnostic test for depression is nothing so comforting, so linear and clean as a blood test. It is a visual assessment of behaviour, and a judgement call. It is a label wrapped around us, inside which we might comfort or lose ourselves as we choose.

Five of the nine symptoms are sufficient to do the job. Depression is not a disease of the brain, though it may correlate with or possibly sometimes be contributed to or caused by such diseases. It is a condition of the mind. A mind and a brain are different things.

74

One is a physical object, which can be seen and – at least when no longer nestled in a living skull doing its mundane and mystical work – touched and weighed and smelled. A mind is a metaphysical concept, more than the sum of its physical parts; a thing beyond the things of which it is comprised. When you receive a diagnosis of depression, you are essentially being told that your mind (a metaphysical concept, which you cannot hold or smell or shove in a sling until its broken structure fuses back together) is not working properly, and that you must take these physical drugs to remedy it. And yet therapy is also routinely recommended – we understand that there is a role for the mind in the treatment of our bodies – that we can, through our thoughts and decisions, make things better. We can make them worse too.

For many people, antidepressants make a real and important difference to depression, as in the case of my friend; but how can they do this, when standard forms of mild depression are not physically detectable by any more scientific method than observation, mostly as reported by non-experts like the patient and their loved ones? In light of this, proposing a solely material solution to an immaterial problem seems slightly insane, though of course you cannot safely say as much to a psychiatrist. There is an inherent insanity in a patient dangling that word about like an exhausted yo-yo on a limp string in a psychiatrist's office. When you're the one being assessed or diagnosed, using the word 'insane' is like roaring 'MACBETH' backstage at a production of Shakespeare. Psychiatrists are terrifyingly powerful individuals and can, in extreme cases, hold the keys to one's freedom in the name of 'sanity', a concept whose definition alters based on the norms and habits of the time in which it happens to be applied.

Years after I got myself up off the floor, I read a paper called 'Religion and Madness' written by my doctoral supervisor and mentor, the philosopher David Berman, on how we might distinguish the difference between sane and insane religious belief. I spent many hours with Professor Berman discussing minds, brains and the field he calls psychological philosophy. Many of the questions I carry with me still are questions that arose from our sessions. He was one of the people who helped me – possibly without realising it – back to sanity myself.

The paper references Maurice 'Con' O'Connor Drury, the Irish psychiatrist who wrote of a woman who tried to have her husband declared insane because he had determined to give away all of his (and consequently her) material possessions. Drury could find no evidence that the man was insane, telling the wife that her husband was consciously and with awareness making a decision which would materially disadvantage him, but that he did so happily and with full ability to grasp the consequences. The woman was, perhaps understandably, not happy. One couldn't blame her if she felt less altruistically inclined than her husband. How nebulous the line between what we think of as sanity and its opposite, or its absence, truly is.

So much of mental illness is theoretical, invisible, incongruous and intangible. We cannot find it or cut it out and heave it roughly into a sterilised dish like a freshly removed gobbet of black, cirrhotic liver. When I was on the floor, and my world was terribly cold and terribly small, and offered me no certainty but my own lack of worth or relevance, I could not point to a part of my body and shout, 'Here! Here is where it hurts! Cut it out! Cauterise it! Medicate it away!'

Yet depression was something that I could feel in my body. Indeed, it was all I could feel in any complex or palpable sense. Everything else felt like a hand grazing the glass of the dirty fishbowl in which I aimlessly and pointlessly floated, suspended in cloudy liquid and removed from the reality of living in the world. And yet, to be labelled and physically medicated at so young an age for an immaterial condition was difficult to reconcile. Though I could only vaguely feel the anger – the medication placed me adjacent to my own emotions in a way that gave me some temporary distance from them but also disconnected me further from the world around me – I do know that it made me angry.

The certainty of everyone around me in the face of what I considered such untenable nebulosity was frightening. To be so sure about the nature of something which, when deconstructed even a little, was nearly impossible to explain, trace or locate, seemed an act itself devoid of lucidity or understanding. I did what was recommended and took the medication, but I did so because when you are on fire, you avail of a fire extinguisher. I did not want to subsist within this vacuum of desolation and futility and, at least at that time, I wanted to feel normal again, without a thick, gauzy filter blurring everything into oblivion, more than I wanted to die. Depression, for me, came in part from anger – either as cause or correlate – and a sense of having nowhere healthy to direct it.

Before the diagnosis, I had been angry for years, and the anger felt like truth, so I presumed that it was. It was, to use that tired phrase people generally roll out when their account of reality clashes with everyone else's, 'my truth'. It related in some cases to things that were objectively true – the absence of my father, mistreatment of my mother by my grandmother, lack of money, a bad relationship with my brother, fear, displacement, low self-esteem, a lack of social skills, all the usual emotive descriptors you will find tacked onto the miserable or unstable origin stories of the poor, the chagrined and the mentally perturbed. There was so much to be angry about, for myself and for my mother, who I felt a misguided need to protect, which was in itself not a healthy impulse.

I grew up with the powerful sense that I could not rely on anyone except my mother. I had the capacity to identify wrongdoing around me but, like all children, no power to do anything about it. So I was angry. Angry that my sense of morality appeared to be different from that of some of the adults around me. Angry that everything seemed so unstable and yet my future — like that of most kids with absent fathers – appeared carved into stone tablets that I could never overwrite, for all I tore and bloodied my fingers clawing at them. Depression is a rational response to living through childhood with a perpetual sense of threat and ambiguity, combined with the counter-intuitive sense, common in youth, that nothing can ever change for the better because I had observed it to be the case that almost nothing had so far.

Depression was a kind of change but I did not precisely notice it slithering into me, or rather out from some central place within my depths, because it was not 'done' to me. I did not catch it from a squalid environment, like a toddler licking a tacky handrail on the bus, or pick it up like a virus when shaking a stranger's hand. I did not swallow or inhale it, smoke it or catch it from a toilet seat, as girls I went to school with insisted was true of pregnancy or chlamydia. Depression, whatever it is, was manufactured somewhere dank and mysterious within me; brought forth from my metaphysical mind or my physical brain or both; a mysterious miasma that filled me up from within until I was immersed in dark, dirty water, and no light could get in, and no hope could escape or find oxygen.

It was a perpetual plague, blocking my ability to do things, or to think myself capable of doing them, which is the same thing, really. And yet, all along I have understood that it is not – like a bacterial infection – the illness created by my body's reaction to a malevolent foreign invader. My depression came from me. I had manufactured it – or at least fed it – myself, unwillingly, unconsciously. It was as much part of or dependent upon me as the body I live in. It was as much mine and as much me as any other physical or non-physical part of me. It could not be separated from 'me' (again, whatever that means) any more than my heart, or my brain, or the tissues that quiver and slime, the cells that live and perpetually replace themselves, inside my red depths.

To manage or overcome depression is to manage or overcome the worst tendencies of oneself. At nineteen, I understood this to some extent, but not completely. I had no idea how to respond to or quiet a voice I recognised as my own, or as the voice of ultimate truth or something terrifyingly irresistible telling me every living moment that I was worthless, worthless, worthless. I was a passive, weak, useless expanse of effluent, unworthy to look another person in the eye, unworthy of improvement, deserving only of the torture that played out inside the infuriating limitations of my own soft, weak, insignificant body.

It presented sometimes as physical pain. A memory or an image would push to the front of my slow mind like a person with a grudge wading through livid water, and I would physically flinch. An early precursor to shouting at myself at the sink. Strangers would look and shrink away from this so universal a marker of mental instability, and I would think, *Yes. I would shrink away too, but I can't.* There is, I would think then, no possible route back from here. I'm lost to myself. This is how it will be until it ends or I can no longer bear the noise and the confinement and the terrible distance between my internal environment and the world outside my skin.

There was a way back, but I would find it only with help, work, effort and thought over time, and I would lose a chunk of my youth to the endeavour of feeling my way through the dark while my healthier peers seemed mostly to be feeling one another. It seemed to me by the most charitable interpretation as though others my age began the race to wherever we were all going at zero, while I started at minus two. I would have to work harder than they did just to make it to a starting point they seemed to have long since left behind. This feeling is common in undergraduate students I have since taught who have difficulties that set them a little apart, like dyslexia, autism, mental health issues. Of course it was not 'people my age' but people my age in the environment of an elite university.

It is also common to students I've taught who came, like me, from a working-class home into a vaunted academic environment that is far from meaningfully inclusive, and where there are necessary ways of tacitly signalling belonging that are completely alien to these students. This failure to signal as expected registers as a failure to conform and sets them apart. It left me feeling confused and deeply inadequate. As an undergraduate struggling in this way, the belief that this race to catch up would be what my life looked like made me angry – more with myself than with others, though I had a lot of anger towards some of the people who had made my upbringing and adolescence more than necessarily unstable and unhappy. This anger would take significant time to understand and set aside.

I was enraged by my own inadequacies, like a first-timer at the gym who feels furious when they discover the counter-intuitive limitations of an unfit body grown soft by lack of use. Sometimes, anger is fuel in the short term but it is always ultimately destructive unless understood and its place as primary motivator is eventually given over to something kinder and better intended. When left to its own devices, anger is unmanageable, self-fuelling, and dominates all around it. It is as well to set fire to one room of your house, shut the door and hope it doesn't spread. Not a constructive long-term plan.

Even after a diagnosis of a condition like depression, there are perils to navigate. Diagnosis is usually talked about as a challenging but positive step; a sort of nascence – the beginning stages of positivity; growth out of what feels like an internal death. It is, in more ways than seem apparent at first, a tender beginning, but it is also a dangerous place to be, prompting a rapid revision of your self-image when you are still maximally vulnerable. Reading a list of symptoms or hearing them described by a doctor can give a person who has collapsed around their own suffering a sense of something to grip and use to pull themselves upright. It can quickly and easily become a person's central characteristic. We have most of us witnessed someone who becomes confined within the label of their disorder, or condition, or set of conditions. Always, solidity eludes when discussing mental health. A name is given to a set of behaviours, a name like depression, and you may find yourself using phrases like 'as a person with depression, I think/do/believe X'. Worse still is to think or say, 'as a person with depression, I am incapable of Y'.

A diagnosis can be comforting because it makes the state in which we find ourselves retrospectively appear determined, and therefore not our fault. It can be stultifying and frightening because it makes our future decisions and fortunes appear equally predetermined, and therefore outside our control. We can be set adrift in the shadow of a new name by which we are expected to define ourselves, and by which others will sometimes define us. It is essential to hold fast to the idea that outcomes are not ultimately decided by the condition. There is freedom even within what can feel like the restraint of that label. It should, like any label placed upon you by the world outside, be worn loosely at best. It took me several years to manage and understand the state of being that the label alludes to without defining myself by it completely.

It is not, though it may appear immediately around diagnosis, the missing and true context to your life, and the complete explanation for why you have struggled. It might be the partial explanation, or it may simply be an outcome of the fact that you have struggled. Too mysterious and opaque for us to be confidently sure of its essential nature – if it has one – depression is simply another element of our unique and differentiated experience which we are obliged to navigate. It is not a gift of specialness; a virtue to use as an excuse to disengage from the mundanity and excitement of participating in the world, nor a revealed truth; a punishment from on high to feel angry about. It is not secret knowledge. It simply *is*, whatever it is.

The lie depression tells is that we are nothing without it. That even as it tells us the worst possible story, it reveals the truth. About ourselves, the world, the future. It trickles slowly in, filling us with its dark, bitter, liquid arrogance and shame, splitting and eroding everything it passes through, emptying us out. It can make us feel insane, bereft, abandoned. It can convince us that there is nothing of us left to retrieve, or nothing of us worth retrieving. The fact that our bodies – our minds – are capable of generating this complex state of being does not mean that this is all we are. Having felt this way does not mean we will feel this way again or that we will always feel this way. Depression is a descriptive label, not a prophesy. There can be an 'after'.

3

Neurodiverse

This very heart which is mine will forever remain indefinable to me. Between the certainty I have of my existence and the content I try to give to that assurance, the gap will never be filled. Forever I shall be a stranger to myself. In psychology as in logic, there are truths but no truth.

— Albert Camus, *The Myth of Sisyphus*

WHY DO SO MANY therapists speak in a tone that suggests they're shoeing a horse and you're the horse? Millennials and Gen Z are the most therapised generations after all, so we should know. The therapist is aiming not to spook you while they peer beyond whatever facade you walk in with at what's going on beneath, I suppose, which is why I find this particular therapist emitting a soft tutting noise somewhat thrilling. It is, unmistakably, a tut. Like a farrier surveying a scruffy piebald who's been traversing cobbles unshod for the entirety of its life. This is our first appointment together and I take a moment to have a light gloat over the fact that she's probably not supposed to do that. The sound is one you might make when beckoning to a stray cat in a foreign country or gently lamenting a small injustice. Like the inflection prompted upon being handed a flat white with a slightly loose to-go lid so that warm milk dribbles stickily into the hollow of your thumb on your way to work. It isn't a tragedy but it's not great either. Not an optimal beginning.

A soft, barely voluntary little tut. A scoff, really. One of those luxury scoffs that escapes you in the privacy of a less self-aware moment. Sure aren't you lucky to be having fancy little coffees or bearing witness to the sweet, canny face of a disinterested foreign street cat at all? Somewhere in your mind twitches the knowledge that you're not really entitled to be upset when the milk spills or the imperious cat who doesn't understand English won't befriend you. It's all a bit . . . indulged. All a bit 'most therapised generation'. Some people don't even have access to to-go lids for their fancy little coffees. Most people, and certainly most therapists, would have muffled the scoff. This person isn't bound by the conventions of politeness or, arguably, professionalism. That is either an excellent sign or very much the opposite. I imagine I'll find out in time.

This therapist is new and comes highly recommended as a specialist in this area. I did the research. I always do the research. It's a defensible way of justifying procrastination. It's taken me a year since the diagnosis to finally find someone with space in their appointment book and expertise, then to arrange this appointment in the begrudging awareness that it might be good for me. Or rather, that I could be doing myself some sort of disservice by neglecting to get on with it. To deal actively rather than passively with this information I had been given about myself, like an elaborate gift that's too heavy to walk home with, or a ticking briefcase. Information conveyed in an obscenely solemn tone suggesting that it may kick up all sorts of dust from my past. It would probably reconstitute my present and prompt a new conception of my future, went the suggestion. There may be a bit of an unravelling, went the warning, so I should prepare for a veil to be lifted or a new lens to be fitted, perhaps. Either way, the world would likely begin to look suddenly very different indeed.

Right so. I'll put 'deal with that' on the old to-do list. But then, everything had changed regardless. I've lived out of a suitcase in three countries over the course of this year. As I focused on getting my life together, I could only marvel at everything falling (what felt) arbitrarily asunder around me. This new label in a world and history replete with labels barely made a dent. If anything I felt wary of the new lens rather than eager to reinterpret everything recast through the light it refracted.

For six months last year I ate my dinner each night from atop an upturned cardboard box in a dingy, completely unfurnished flat. It was a fitting place to pass this non-consensual lacuna while we waited for delayed Australian visas. Everything had gone kind of wrong all at once. We were supposed to be enjoying a lingering valediction with my family in Ireland but suddenly had to return to London for a variety of reasons and, having nowhere to live and being eager for a short lease, we took what we could afford under our unusual circumstances, as you do when you're stuck.

The flat festered menacingly in a building which doubled as a home office for drug dealers who valued anonymity, and industrious freelance prostitutes in one of London's neglected, depressing post-war satellite towns in which everything is made of mildewed concrete; where people live hard lives and look older than they really are. The railway station across the road from the building featured a billboard encouraging people to 'seek help' rather than 'disappearing' either by suicide or, presumably, just downing tools, throwing their SIM card onto the obliging tracks, and getting out of Dodge. You won't find that sort of billboard (or any billboard for that matter) in wealthy neighbourhoods. Not much call for them in Foxrock or Belgravia or the Hamptons. On average, people checking out of their lives and dissolving into the atmosphere seems to be less of a problem in those places. I thought of advertising posters I'd passed the week before in Kensington and Chelsea's Sloane Square Underground station. One was for organic, grain-free dog food, another for a high-end interiors website. On the train platform next to our apartment building, damp posters advertised local wrestling events, Iceland supermarket deals and fast food.

In our unfurnished apartment across the street from the sign overlooking the railway line, located over a Twenty-Four-Hour Fitness with broken mirrors and a takeaway pizza restaurant with windows permanently furred by condensation and a distinct ambience of money laundering about it, we sat on the floor to eat each evening, the cheap weave of the scabrous, frayed carpet biting hungrily through my trousers and into the soft flesh of my backside. It felt (from the waist down, anyway) like a return to the financial strain and anxiety of my childhood. That burning backslide across coarse carpet that everyone who grew up poor spends their adulthood in perpetual terror of.

Now that we are finally settled in Australia after the most tumultuous eighteen months of my life, this seems like a sufficiently bedlam-free time to consider the label I've been carrying about for a year in silence and with a lot of unanswered questions. It wasn't a purposeful secrecy. Just the kind which arises from understanding that people will have questions and will likely expect me to provide answers to those questions. That's fair enough, but I don't have them, and so I pocketed the label with the others and take it out in quiet moments from time to time, feeling its weight, turning it over in my hands and peering at it. Checking the fit.

Each time, I put it away again, dissatisfied with the sense of ambiguity and incompleteness it carries. Conscious that if I wore it publicly, I would doubtless become subject to the narrow assumptions it generates and the sprawling vagueness it attempts to encapsulate. That's a fitting word, bedlam, evoking that famous London madhouse. Like all such places, it was somewhere to put people who everyone else didn't quite know what to do with. Not just people who were dangerous to themselves or others, but people who couldn't conform, or simply elected not to because all of it comes down to madness in the end. The ones who make us uncomfortable in a way that could be our problem or theirs (but making it theirs is tidier).

These days there are hardly fewer people we don't know what to do with but the modern malaise tends to pathologise otherness rather than moralise over it – a relatively recent approach. Until the mid-twentieth century, epileptic seizures were still considered a sign of moral contagion, possession or proximity to evil. In the US several states prevented people with epilepsy from marrying and some encouraged their sterilisation in a misguided and authoritarian effort to prevent the dissemination of what was ultimately a long-vilified medical condition. Prefrontal lobotomy won the Nobel Prize in 1949 for Dr Egaz Moniz, who designed the procedure. It was used to treat conditions and symptoms as disparate as those from schizophrenia and 'melancholia' to what we'd characterise today as severe social anxiety. It was George Washington University's Dr Walter Freeman who performed the procedure on more than 3,500 patients with his 'ice-pick' method. Around 50,000 people underwent lobotomies between 1949 and 1952 alone. Ultimately, the procedure was a pseudoscientific method of rendering difficult people more passive and has thankfully fallen from its former position of scientific respectability into the ignominy it always merited. It seems Freeman thought there were few aberrant or socially unacceptable behaviours that couldn't be mediated with a quick ice pick to the brain. I imagine he was correct about that.

Perhaps you'd noticed but some of the people who struggle, or don't quite fit, or feel existentially at odds with the pace and norms of contemporary living are called autistic now. Some are considered to have ADHD. Sometimes both. These two labels in particular are increasingly common, with rates of diagnosis in adulthood rapidly increasing in recent years. In the mid-1980s researchers at the University of Utah and UCLA conducted an autism epidemiology study among children and reported the prevalence of autism as four in ten thousand using the relevant diagnostic criteria at that time. Now the number is one in thirty-six. There was a 787 per cent reported rise in the number of autism diagnoses of children in the UK between 1998 and 2018.

A brief toilet-scroll through social media is sufficient to reveal the quicksand of public dialectic on this topic.

Some people dismiss increased diagnoses among children and adults as a sign of progress resulting from more experts in the area and greater access to diagnosis. Autism and ADHD rates were always this high; people were simply struggling by without diagnosis or support. Simple as that. Others consider the explosive rate of increase as symptomatic of a lucrative industry in neurodivergence, in which clinicians with constantly widening diagnostic criteria are professionally and financially incentivised to define an increasingly vast suite of human behaviours, traits and tendencies as autism, or ADHD, or both.

When I contacted a leading Dublin clinic specialising in adult autism diagnosis to ask how many of the people who walk through their door for assessment walk out with an autism diagnosis, they responded that while they didn't have the numbers to hand, 'the majority of people who come to us feeling that they are Autistic are correct and leave with an identification/diagnosis'. With assessment costs often running potentially into the thousands and extensive wait times, this is not a process anyone undertakes lightly. Most autism is diagnosed in childhood, so undiagnosed adults may have experienced social, functional, behavioural, medical or other difficulties which were framed differently by those around them throughout their lives. According to Irish autism charity As I Am, 85 per cent of autistic people in Ireland are either unemployed or underemployed.

It may simply not have occurred to people who have grown up feeling that they are the problem that they are autistic, given that public understanding of autism is poor and conversation around autism in adults (and particularly in women) is only now becoming more prevalent. It is also certainly the case that many adults who are seriously considering that they may be autistic will generally conduct careful research into autism and therefore may never get as far as assessment if that research tells them the shoe doesn't fit.

Labels attached to autism and ADHD, which fall under the umbrella of what is generally referred to as 'neurodivergence', are being applied to enough people whom we don't otherwise know what to do with or how to categorise that it constitutes what we might call a trend. People whose 'otherness' we had no particular name for up to now. This psychological zeitgeist carries with it a simultaneous fashion for and scepticism about neurodivergence as well as a thriving industry in diagnostic and support services. That is undeniable. The recognition that there is not simply one 'type' of brain is undoubtedly a form of progress. It creates breathing room for the people who are simply different or a little bit 'other' without moralising over that difference or prompting social, religious or surgical (as in Freeman's day) impetus to 'correct' or 'reroute' them toward the 'objectively' correct (neurotypical) way to be, according to general consensus.

Yet trends always meet collective needs and articulate cultural moments. The neurodivergence conversation brings with it the same flattening and discouragement of questioning that arises when anything becomes an albeit contested part of the status quo. 'Autistic' is a label easily used to flatten a person's complexity and agency, and to dismiss them. It is unarguably a condition which precedes any ontology or attempt to name it. In its more severe forms, it can be very distinctive, resulting in people who simply cannot meld invisibly into public life in ways that make their passage through the world extremely challenging.

My cousin in childhood had no speech but would sit for hours watching the washing machine agitating laundry round and round in endless, rapt focus if left to do it. When his mother attempted to move him – because he needed to eat or sleep or simply engage in other activities, his rage and distress were those of a child whose world was unmaking itself around him. He would very easily become overwhelmed or overstimulated by noise, and as a little girl I found him both frightening and incomprehensible. Or my friend's adult brother, who doesn't really speak much – and remained completely silent for years – but who I sat watching in fascinated admiration at her wedding party. At 2 or 3 a.m., when the last song was being played and everyone had left the dance floor to trail off to bed, footsore and intoxicated, there he was, sober as a housecat and dancing alone on the dance floor, utterly lost inside the music and completely unselfconscious. There was nothing performative in it. He was simply doing what felt good in the moment, immune to the gaze of others. I wished I were more like him. There is no doubt that the label of autism is deeply necessary – it provides a bridge by which a unique, different and rich experience of the world might be translated to those who cannot relate to it and might otherwise fear, condemn or otherwise devalue it. It gives context to both the people who bear the label and those they meet. In this sense, it is self-actualising and empowering, giving voice to that which many people can't or otherwise won't take the time to understand.

It is also a convenient label for some to hide behind or to weaponise as justification for why others need to adapt to and accommodate them and not the other way around. It can be a disempowering label; a route to passivity in a society where group-endorsed specialness is a status symbol and, sometimes, a get-out-of-(social)-jail-free card. It's a label that costs a lot to access through official diagnosis, given that public health services in Ireland and the UK are about as well funded and staffed as most other public services (except for Revenue – somehow those lads never seem to run out of printer ink).

In late 2023 almost 158,000 people in the UK had an open referral for suspected autism. That's a 50 per cent increase from 2022. The median wait time for NHS appointments in 2023 was 300 days. This has created a situation which often allows people with financial means to access diagnosis before those without, and since more severe or pronounced symptoms or traits of autism (difficulty navigating social hierarchies and norms, intense anxiety in group scenarios or crowds, selective mutism or sensitivity to sensory stimuli among them) may make living independently or maintaining a traditional job more difficult, it's possible that people without advocates but with more severe challenges and need are waiting longer for diagnosis, if they can access it at all. In Ireland there are private clinics specialising in both autism and ADHD diagnosis with waiting lists in the years rather than months. When I was curious about the diagnostic process and asked around among a handful of helpful acquaintances who had received a diagnosis in adulthood, the feedback was universal – go private if you ever want to actually have an assessment, and be ready to wait.

As a result of widespread difficulty in accessing diagnosis and our flawed human propensity to read lists of symptoms of various conditions on the internet and confidently declare ourselves infected, afflicted or moribund (no, you probably don't have necrotising fasciitis, it's just a smudge of high-quality printer ink from that threatening letter you received from Revenue), self-diagnosis rates of both autism and ADHD are depressingly high. The result is cohorts of people who identify as neurodivergent without having been diagnosed formally. A quick Google search will reveal a relatively vicious online debate – the sort that people often engage in when they perceive an identity in which they've invested their personhood to be under threat – about the validity of self-diagnosis, especially for those who are struggling and do not have the financial means to access services.

Diagnostic labels clearly possess some appeal, if only as means of explaining or giving a name to the friction so many people feel in navigating the world around them. The cultural conversation around neurodivergence is beginning to have a flavour of those people who say things like 'I'm *sooo* OCD' because they feel irritated when their mother leaves the living room light on or find mild satisfaction in neatly folded laundry. The OCD comment brings to mind the time an academic friend of mine had a student ask for an extension on an essay on the grounds that it was giving her PTSD. He was so shocked by her apparent earnestness that he responded, 'You mean the thing soldiers get after witnessing their friends die?' It is a bizarre example of concept creep in action, where a medical, mental health concept can blur at the borders until it might be used to describe a response to very normal stress rather than exceptional and legitimate trauma. There's nothing of substance in this sort of flippant pathologisation of utterly commonplace human feeling, but there is something bigger going on in phrasing that locates validity of feeling and central elements of identity within what is considered, medically speaking, a disorder.

By this understanding, we do not *have* something. We are not influenced or challenged *by* something. Rather, we *are* something. And after all, we can none of us help what we are. If I *am* something, then some manner of immutability is implied. A genetic destiny fructified or an environmental harm enacted against me. A switch flipped from inside or outside and for which I am not answerable. A substrate from which I am sprung forth. I am the end result of a causal process that is ultimately (frighteningly, comfortingly) out of my hands. I can let go of the friction that arises from feeling a need to resist my own impulses or challenge my own behaviours. I can release a little bit of my precious agency, like a caged bird.

I can't, obviously. None of us can. We're not caged birds – or at least in this sense not caged by others – but the fact is that many of us would kind of *like* to be. Just a little and just sometimes. Wrestling with oneself is a primary activity of being alive and a perpetually laborious, boring and annoying one. It's difficult and usually feels bad, and even when you win you still often feel like there's nothing to show for it. That is self-actualisation, though, and it is quite different from emotional resolution, which is often what we go to therapy to find. We want to feel better now, sometimes even at the cost of our own agency. In one way or another, we nurse a longing to be exonerated of responsibility for our own flaws and make a life in the cage while still reserving the right to resent the fact of our being stuck in there.

Back in the session with the new therapist, as I sit on the Zoom call (of course we're not having an in-person therapy session – that's all very analogue in a post-Covid world), I can't help but suspect that such labels may be more hindrance than help to me. If autism in particular sits along a spectrum, then I'm not on the serious end of it. I'm not someone whose everyday route through the world is terminally impeded by the ways in which I just can't and don't process the world as neurotypical people do. If I am what you'd call autistic (and I certainly do exhibit many of the traits observed in autistic women), I'm more of a stealth agent among the normies, like many autistic women with their famed tendency to 'mask' (repress their natural behaviours and inclinations and ultimately simulate those of others to get by and maintain harmony in company). Data-chugging to learn how things work in new social hierarchies and the behaviours people generally expect, particularly of women, and then doing those things in order to smooth my way through. The literature calls it masking, and yet, to an extent, everyone is doing this in social contexts. Most of us moderate our behaviour around others in line with social and contextual expectation. Some people can't do it, and their lives are objectively harder. Some people choose not to do it, or to do it less, and their lives are also harder. We don't lobotomise them any more though, which is a sort of progress. Does the label 'autistic' being attributed to a person like me in some way diminish or render more difficult the experience of those autistic people who cannot mask, cannot pass, cannot blend to get ahead or even get by? Maybe.

When I look at a list of indicators of autism in women and men (and the diagnostic criteria in the *DSM-5-TR*) I'm not sure they're prescriptive rather than loose descriptions of observed behaviours and inclinations when it comes to people like me who might come across as a bit . . . odd. Or 'off' if we're being ungenerous, which people certainly can be. They're not impenetrable physical facts of the matter like a splintered bone in a swelling leg or a dearth of white blood cells, but stories that explain or describe otherness in ways that pathologise it. Metaphysics in a lab coat. In my case, anyway. In many cases of people who struggle to fit or feel comfortable but know that taking to the dance floor alone isn't socially acceptable and will make life harder.

I'm not sure what it means for me to be autistic, except to be how I've been up to now with the addition of more confident, narrower judgement (justified or otherwise) and possibly marginally more generosity on the part of other people. My aloofness – for which I've been criticised since I was old enough to stare rudely at people without speaking when disinclined – ceases to be rude because it is transmogrified (in the perception of others) into something I can't help. A quirk or a symptom. Evidence of a brain that isn't wired like the others. And yet, that's quite patronising. A survey of autistic people by As I Am reported that 83 per cent of respondents said they felt they 'had to change who they are in order to receive the same chance to participate in day-to-day activities within society'. I'm not someone just in from Jupiter who hasn't yet figured out how the rules work. I usually *can* help it. Any social, professional or other success I've had has largely been gained through electively *helping it* when it serves me to do so. Some might call it masking but that's only part of the story. Rudeness, as it's often interpreted, is just easier sometimes. More honest. And while we're being honest, more personally rewarding in the short term. More natural, perhaps.

Because sometimes you can't be arsed to perform or the cost of doing it in the moment is higher than the cost of electing not to. And because people do interesting things when you look at them without speaking. That one is not to be underestimated. It is a powerful social tool in a world where most people appear to struggle with silence. Look at a person without speaking. Stretch languidly, comfortably into the unfolding silence like a cat in a sun puddle. People tend to unfold or unravel before you and, frankly, there's power in prompting them to do that, particularly in social contexts when, like me, you often feel like you're doing one of those slow, humiliating falls down a small flight of stairs just by being in the room. Silence is subversive somehow. It's a way of collecting inform- ation about a person that is simply less work than verbal digging. It's less work than trying. I'm not sure whether that's autism or the much more relatable and universal state of just being a bit of a dick when you're low on motivation, tired, overwhelmed or lacking internal resources (not to mention low on desire to be liked or any wish to prioritise the immediate comfort of others at the expense of your own).

There are times, particularly in a group, when I will indeed feel slightly overwhelmed, go quiet and retreat into myself. The proverbial 'they' call this a 'shutdown'. I don't see, however, how it would help at all to think of this as something that happens *to* me – as a process in which I have absolutely no agency. It might make me feel better about engaging in a behaviour other people think of as weird or hostile, but not in a way that is ultimately self-actualising. If I embrace this pathology as an umbrella term under which all those sorts of behaviours and several other less socially unac- ceptable ones rest, am I relinquishing my agency? Am I exonerating myself from the duty and privilege of considering the needs of others as highly as I consider my own? Am I making excuses for myself? Am I (dare I say it) just being a bit of a dick? Or am I reacting to a world which demands that I make more effort than other people in the room to be able to connect with them by their preferred means?

The therapist and I go through my history and I find myself intensely bored, which is a sure sign that I've started to drift. It feels from where I'm sitting as though she should notice that – that it's in the job spec – but there are forty minutes left so I suppose we're both just in this now. According to the diagnostic criteria, symptoms of autism must have been present in childhood and remain present through to adulthood for an adult to be considered autistic. We skim over my childhood and love of Jane Austen in adolescence (her world featured appealing, intractable, comprehensible social norms and rules which didn't require parsing or interpretation) until we arrive at the present version. Again I wonder, is this autism or is this just the adult who necessarily results when you're raised in a home that closes ranks around an addict as a form of damage control and you don't ever quite get socialised, like an 'outdoor' dog suddenly brought shivering and wide-eyed inside a house? He'll look without recognition at a sofa or a fridge and have no conceptual context at all for what he is looking at. Therefore, he'll have no means of figuring it out until experience teaches him, first through observation.

There is this ambivalent, dust-kicking, question-raising side to therapy, depending on the methodology a therapist uses. Joan Didion wrote that 'we tell ourselves stories in order to live' and I think of that line whenever I'm faced with the sanguine gaze of a therapist and their soft, interrogative, 'gently, gently shoe the horse' tone. Hastening slowly. Surveying the territory. Pressing mildly here and there to find where the tenderness is. Little taps of the hammer – no sudden jolts. Searching, searching. Not tutting or scoffing as far as they can help it, but then we're all human and there's so very much to scoff at. The confidential, supplicating whisper of the confessional, where you reprise your role as patient-penitent, and they theirs as therapist-priest. You talk and talk, peel and reveal until you find a version of the story you can live with. Some people seek absolution in therapy but some therapists don't have enough of the priest in them. Without an element of challenge, pushback, some hard truths, some uncomfortable self-assessment, there is only validation of feeling and experience. We all need some of that, but without the other, absolution is mere delusion. Succour at the expense of perspective. Comforting, righteous ignorance.

We do tell ourselves stories in order to live. Or we enable ourselves to make sense of being alive through the stories we tell. We arrange the past and present into comprehensible shapes that are decipherable to us and that place us in the best or worst light (wherever we've been taught to assume we belong), and we predict the future based on these. We locate themes within past stories in which we feature, and we construct a theory of self around them.

We tell ourselves that this is not *a* story but *the* story. The reality of how things are. An implacable

'I' emerges – an entity that has something essential and inexorably in common with every version of itself from the one who ate half a garden snail at the age of five (that's a bit old, like, maybe you should have known better?) to the one who graduated university or who occasionally remembers the time they read the word 'orgasm' instead of 'organism' aloud in biology class at fourteen and to this day the knees still almost go from under them.

A few months before the autism diagnosis, I spent about twenty minutes talking with psychotherapist and psychologist Esther Perel in the kitchen of a house in London on a heavy summer evening. The back door was ajar for people who wanted to wander in and out, smoking and laughing and eating olives. It was something of an out-of-body experience. Perel is probably the world's best known and undoubtedly most utterly beloved psychotherapist and psychologist. She told me something in that slightly breathy and melodic, distinctly Belgian voice which reverberates regularly through my bathroom – because I usually listen to her therapy session podcasts *Where Should We Begin?* when I take a morning shower, but I didn't tell her as much because that might seem unhinged.

In those sessions, Perel masterfully sees beyond the obvious and identifies the stories that people use to trip themselves up, as we all do. She challenges, supports and nudges people encouragingly as they find their own route to a workable story. She frequently asks whether a theory she puts forward resonates with her patient, saying that she has no idea if it's true. She also has the benefit of rarely sounding as though she is shoeing a skittish horse.

Perel told me that the therapeutic model rests on the idea that our past determines our present but that the same does not have to follow of the future. She said she didn't know if it was incontrovertibly true. That none of us does. She is right. If we have agency, it has to come in somewhere in this causal chain, an unmoved mover. The seed of something miraculous that allows us to notice the pattern, say 'Fucking stop it!' and initiate some change. Of course, whether this agency exists, and where and how it is generated, is the sort of septic vortex of a question that philosophers have time for but nobody else wants to touch on account of possessing moderate sanity and wanting to leave an hour free in the evening to watch Netflix and make eye contact with their families. But we are obliged to presume it's true in order to get anything done. So we do precisely that.

The whole therapeutic model rests on the idea that we are where we are based on a murky soup of genetics, socio-economics, environmental influences and choice, and that we can volitionally change if we want to. We do this by closely examining and reconstructing the stories we tell ourselves 'in order to live'. Not just the story of how we got to our particular 'here' (e.g. hyperventilating in a therapist's virtual office because supermarkets, with their darting cheese-grabbers and their canned pop music from 2008, make us feel so stressed that we keep forgetting basic things and then ironically having to return eight or nine times a week for milk or beans or whatever else) but also of our potential to be different. If that's not the case, then therapy is the emotional equivalent of paying someone with an accreditation on their office wall to batter you with a stick dipped in the effluent of all the worst things that ever happened to you and all the worst things you've ever done.

In therapy, you learn to tell new versions of these central stories – more helpful ones. I sometimes think that this is a form of self-delusion, but then so were the initial stories we lived by, and those are generally crafted for us by others. You weren't an inherently bad child, goes the new story, you were responding to the circumstances of your upbringing in a way that enabled you to cope with them, so your misbehaviour wasn't weakness but fortitude and self-preservation. Maybe this version of events will help you to consider your parents' choices differently or find it easier to see value in yourself.

Sometimes the stories exonerate us, and sometimes that creates new problems. That relationship didn't end because he went out of his way to put himself first. Now you think of it, you never actually told him what you needed but held him accountable regardless when he failed to intuit it. You crave intimacy but you're also terrified of it. He wasn't the first, either. Whoopsie! Work to do there, then. Like the famously nebulous and underwhelming Fianna Fáil election slogan that both incensed and entertained the nation of Ireland in 2002: 'A Lot Done. More to Do.' It reads like something a teacher might write on a report card when there are too many kids in the class to precisely recall whose progress this one refers to. It's the kind of thing you tell yourself when you've missed all your deadlines and have absolutely no intention of catching up now but would still very much like to save face if you can help it. Plausible deniability.

For a person who is sceptical about the ideas that form the bases of therapeutic methodologies, I've done a lot of therapy. Of course I have. A background in philosophy will ensure that you need therapy even if you didn't before you ever read a word of Plato and set yourself on a path to realising that we are – all of us, especially the most confident – utterly, ineffably clueless about almost everything. Now, the therapist interrupts my wandering thoughts by asking what sort of therapy I've done before. We're still evaluating me, it seems. Her face, carefully arranged into a passive expression, implies that she isn't judging. But she is evaluating, and that's really the same thing without the potential prison sentence at the end.

'Cognitive behavioural therapy, mostly,' I reply, squinting past her as one always does in a therapist's office to see if I can redress the power imbalance I'm feeling by finding evidence of her personal shortcomings through objects or books displayed on her shelves. My eyes catch on a copy of Prince Harry's *Spare* and one of those battery-powered dancing sunflowers like a fingertip feeling around a roll of Sellotape for the edge. That'll do.

'Oh that's very bad for us,' she says. 'Not at *all* ideal for us.' The soft tutting recommences while I reply robotically, 'Well actually I found much of it quite helpful . . .' I found its roots in Stoic philosophy and radical sense of ownership very meaningful when I felt weakest and most afraid. It's an approach that allows an individual to focus on whatever they can control and change rather than the many things that they really can't. A tiny silence shimmers out from the screen while she partitions my words and wedges into the space between them. 'I'm glad to hear it,' she replies, smiling thinly but looking a little as though she isn't really at all glad to hear it and clearly we'll have a lot of deconditioning to do. 'We're conditioned to think that CBT works for everyone,' she says, 'but it takes a prescriptive approach that doesn't always include people like us and can seek solutions in attempting to force us down neurotypical routes.' I blink slowly, feeling like a cat when they make that strange open-mouthed sniffing investigation of something weird they've happened to find under the bed. I googled it once after wondering if my friend's cat Greg was having a stroke. He wasn't, and it's called the Flehmen response. They do it when they want to get their vomer-onasal organ involved in whatever is going on if something doesn't seem right or usual. Greg was just trying to bring order to chaos. I sympathised.

'You should maybe immerse in this process,' a pocket of my recently termed autistic brain interjects gingerly. 'Are you protecting yourself by not immersing? You think a therapist can't read past your faux-intellectual persiflage? You're paying for this, dullard. You're not twelve. She's the therapist and you're the 'tism-riddled ding-dong.' And it's tempting, as the therapist describes what she imagines to be my experience, to adopt someone else's account of my internal world. Their story of my mechanics. Because I've felt the rusty grind of the cogs juddering, clutching and catching where I imagine things could potentially roll smoothly, every waking moment of my life. A sense that perhaps I'm missing something important here in almost every inter-action with other people.

To demur now, to absorb this new story, would be so soothing. Moonlight on still water. A cup of warm milk clutched in a child's chubby little starfish hands. It would feel like surrendering to something bigger and give me that lens through which to understand myself and the world. A sort of meaning, and, with Nietzsche's God dead as skinny jeans, don't we all need a spot of that? So why not? Well ... because there's more to an individual than any single identity label, and this one is distinctly pinching under the arms.

'People like us can have a hard time working in an office environment,' the therapist says as we talk about my job. That phrase 'people like us' bothers me for some reason. It evokes that feeling of walking quickly past an open door in a loose jacket and being yanked backwards with agonising self-consciousness when the fabric gets caught in the handle. Embarrassment. A tiny flicker of self-directed rage. A longing to be anywhere else.

Perhaps I'm uncomfortable because it's not yet clear to me that we have anything meaningfully in common and her presumption registers as a lack of intellectual curiosity.

That isn't what she means, though. My new therapist means that we are both diagnosed autistic, and presumably she is acting on the belief that because of this, we can presume to share some further, deep commonality of experience. Mutual challenges, perhaps, in navigating what she describes as a 'neurotypical world'? A common neurology, maybe? But doesn't everyone, in some respect or other, move through the world as though their shirt has shrunk in the wash?

Though the diagnostic test for autism is conducted by a clinical psychologist and is descriptive – a question-and-answer affair based on the experience of the person being tested and, when possible, the close family members or friends who have known them since childhood – nobody scanned my brain. The literature suggests that if someone did undergo the faff and expense of conducting such a test using the infrastructure of our already terminally overwhelmed healthcare system, they would find evidence that my functional brain organisation differs from that of what is called a 'neurotypical' person. Or at least that, according to recent research published in *The British Journal of Psychiatry*, there is 'robust evidence that the brains of females and males with ASD are functionally organized differently'. So the brain systems involved in motor, language and visuospatial attention differ in women with ASD (autism spectrum disorder) as opposed to men. And both differ from those of men and women who can be described as neurotypical.

By this definition, autism is evidenced in the differing brain activity of those who are diagnosed with it, but this is not the means by which people are actually diagnosed. After the diagnosis I read everything I could get my hands on. A smartarse would describe this sort of deep-diving as typically autistic, but they can shove off. If a psychologist gives you a socially laden medicalised label claiming your brain function differs from the 'norm' and tells you that it is a major factor in the story of how you came to be where you are and the one you will now construct of where you are going, a bit of reading seems downright sensible. As does asking questions before you absorb an external narrative of who and what you are.

Autism looks very different in women and men, while diagnosis rates are rising in adults and among women in particular. The umbrella of diagnostic criteria widens and as a result, more diverse sorts of people stand together beneath it. The same goes for ADHD, which the new therapist now says breezily she's confident I also have. After a pause in which I say nothing, she adds, 'But I can't assess that formally myself. I can connect you with the right resources, though, if you like?' I'm baffled by the certainty with which she speaks, how easily and casually she labels me – a stranger – after what is now a twenty-something-minute conversation and some online tests she asked me to do before our appointment. This, surely, is not a serious interaction.

When you think of autism, you probably think of a male person – perhaps that nonverbal child wearing noise-cancelling headphones in the bread aisle who won't make eye contact when you have to awkwardly reach past him for the crumpets, or a socially incompetent, taciturn man in creased trousers who is spectacularly unsuccessful on the dating scene. He collects Magic: The Gathering cards and has an unnerving amount of ready knowledge about trains (he's only taciturn until you ask him about trains). Or, if you're particularly badly informed, and a lot of us are, you'll think of a *Rain Man* type.

By this tired assumption, there are broadly two common autistic tropes: weird, kooky, socially inappropriate genius with little inclination to function 'normally'; and weird, unsettling, socially incapable recluse with little capacity to function 'normally'. Both are men or boys. When there's talk of autism, you probably won't think of a woman or girl at all, and if you do, you won't think of a writer who must network with gregarious, socially adept people for work and is extremely particular about who she goes to for highlights.

Autism is categorised as a neurodevelopmental disorder. But as the umbrella broadens, I wonder whether that is an accurate characterisation, especially given the descriptive nature of the diagnostic testing and the fact that another Irish clinic I enquired with informed me that 'nine out of ten' adults who paid them for an autism assessment left with an autism diagnosis. Is this what I, and other relatively high-functioning people who nonetheless carry a belief from childhood that they never quite comfortably fit and sometimes don't want to, have? Is this what we *are*? If a significant and growing proportion of the population broadly falls under this umbrella or possesses traits that do, who is to say that they are abnormal or that something in their neurological development, rather than making some of them a bit aloof and very good at tabletop role-playing games, has gone wrong? This might be a problem with our collective understanding and the story we tell about neurodiversity rather than neurodiverse people (whatever they are) in themselves.

Daniel Kahneman's 2011 book, *Thinking, Fast and Slow* brought awareness of intuitive and deliberative thinking to people outside the field of psychology. Intuitive thinking is the automatic, non-conscious 'implicit processing that is independent of working memory and cognitive ability', according to Mark Brosnan and Chris Ashwin in the journal *Autism,* while deliberative processing 'involves slower, effortful, sequential, conscious, explicit processing and is heavily dependent on working memory and related to individual differences in cognitive ability'. Brosnan and Ashwin argue that this difference is a key one in people with autism and autistic traits. These people, their research suggests, engage 'in (slow) deliberative processing, rather than reflecting normative biases associated with (fast) intuitive processing'.

Brosnan and Ashwin put forward the theory that autistic people tend to use deliberative thinking in situations where the majority of people will use intuitive thinking – the sort of implicit, reactive thought that allows us to make quick decisions but which can involve cutting logical corners. As Kahneman puts it, 'This is the essence of intuitive heuristics: when faced with a difficult question, we often answer an easier one instead, usually without noticing the substitution.' Well, many autistic people apparently notice the substitution. No matter who you are, you will have encountered a disagreement or conversation in which intuitive thinking clashes with deliberative.

Autistic people, it's suggested, tend to utilise the slower, more deliberate form of thinking that most people save for complex problems, a tricky algorithm, or comprehending or constructing a philosophical argument. Cognitively, as it were, autistic people check their work as they go rather than favouring intuitive reasoning, which is something most brains engage in automatically. It's energy- and time-efficient but makes us more likely to commit errors in reasoning and take cognitive shortcuts.

There are disadvantages to thinking deliberatively most or all of the time too, and plenty of them. However, there are also real benefits. The autistic brain is an innovative problem-solver, and it doesn't follow that people with autism cannot think intuitively. Research suggests that many can or can be encouraged to (in the case of children with autism). They simply appear to prefer not to in some cases, or to find a more involved and sometimes labour-intensive process of thought more conducive to reaching the desired level of understanding. And yet, so much is not understood in relation to autistic people and how they interact with the world. Meanwhile, this dearth of knowledge coincides with rising rates of diagnosis. According to Ashwin and Bronson:

> 'Many questions remain concerning the underlying mechanisms related to the reasoning differences in autism. One possibility is that the mechanisms for intuitive processing are impaired in autism, resulting in deliberation being the default and

dominant form of reasoning. If the intuitive mechanisms are impaired, this would lead to pervasive deficits in any processing requiring rapid and unconscious processing across different domains and functioning, such that even if an autistic individual tried to utilise intuitive processing, they would have difficulties in doing so. An alternative possibility is that the mechanisms for intuitive processing are intact, but that autistic individuals do not typically or spontaneously utilise this specific style of reasoning, or that the information processing style in autism does not involve or require intuitive processing.'

This is the key question I carry as a person with an autism diagnosis, and it is a question to which everyone from the layperson on the street to the scoffing therapist seems to have presupposed an answer. Accommodating difference, one could argue, renders irrelevant the fact of the matter of whether my brain is incapable (or less capable) of intuitive reasoning or just better at, or prefers, deliberative reasoning. There is a crucial difference between *this is the only way I can be* and *this is the way I am*. The former is – practically, socially and in some cases officially – considered a disability. The latter is a preference or a strength.

And, of course, we set aside in all this the slightly terrifying implication that neurotypical people appear to be so very deeply awful, on average, at deliberative reasoning – at identifying and generating conclusions that have any logical link to their premises. Which is, I suppose, why I know so many university-educated women who keep crystals in their designer handbags in the hope of being calmer or luckier or whatever. Why so many people's disagreements with their partner over laundry or groceries cede into point-scoring exercises over something unrelated that happened at their work Christmas party nine years ago. Why most people, in a debate over one point, will routinely move the goalposts until they're actually discussing another or refuse to change their mind despite the evidence not going their way. It may explain why conversations under Facebook posts look the way they do and possibly also why the mullet is fashionable again. (That last one might be a stretch but I think there is significant evidence that we haven't thought deliberatively about the mullet.)

As I sit in the therapy session, I think about that. Not the mullet thing, though someone should fund studies into whatever that's about as a matter of the public good. I think about the roots of liberalism, and how the therapeutic tradition has emerged from rationalism. The idea that therapy should not just affirm a person's emotional state but is meant to equip them to see the world through a rational perspective. That radical subjectivity is ultimately disempowering. I think about systems and individuals. Labels and generalisations. Horses and people with weird, velvety voices. Is versus ought. Prince Harry and dancing sunflowers and a small girl who can't have friends over in case her dad turns up drunk and tries to break the door down again, and what her chances of being socially adept ever really were.

I think of the labels I've been handed and instructed to use to describe myself since I was old enough to voice them, and the fact that no matter what I've said about my feelings and experiences in the course of this particular session, this therapist has more or less affirmed them even when they directly contradict concrete statements she has just made as though they are objectively true. All cocoon, no push. All emotion, no rationality. Apart from the scoff, which I respect, but a scoff is unconstructive. There's the issue. I don't need to be swaddled, accepted, told what I am and encouraged to celebrate it. I need help to see how I might help myself. Not with 'self-care' and multivitamins that turn my pee livid yellow and taking note of who 'shows up' for me and constantly repeating that staring weirdly at people and making them uncomfortable just because I can or because I feel like it is great, actually. I need to see myself beyond this one label or any other, because the interior furniture of my mind is what it has always been. I don't need affirmation. Absolution. I need more discomfort. More

121

actualisation. Maybe then I can become someone with the courage to dance by myself.

'Same time again next week?' the therapist asks eventually. The session has ended and she's looking at me curiously, her pen held aloft like the sword of Damocles.

I inhale sharply, considering my answer.

4

Irish

When the soul of a man is born in this country there are nets flung at it to hold it back from flight. You talk to me of nationality, language, religion. I shall try to fly by those nets.
– James Joyce, *A Portrait of the Artist as a Young Man*

I AM FASCINATED BY the concept of 'passing'. In contemporary discourse, the term is commonly used by trans people to characterise the experience of blending in without incongruity. Of minimal disparity between how a person presents themselves as a member of some particular in-group (woman, British, middle-class, whatever) and how others see them. It is the ability to perform elements of our chosen or given identity as perceived by other people – dressing in line with societal expectations or speaking in the correct colloquial lexicon. Looking sufficiently feminine or masculine to meet current standards of femininity or masculinity. It is the optics of belonging. The concept of passing can be applied to more complex judgements we make as well as the ones that are immediately made of or by us. Making the 'correct' cultural references to signal in-group membership. Eating the approved foods as opposed to foods which signal either otherness or disdain for in-group preferences, or both. If I turn up to a vegan lunch club in leather shoes and sweeten my tea with honey brought from home, those around me will quickly judge my commitment to veganism to be spurious. It might provoke their contempt. To pass, you must pass seamlessly. It cannot be a performance involving obvious effort. To belong, you can't be seen to be trying to belong. That is a very difficult bar to meet, especially since we are, all of us, performing. Performance is an inherent feature of belonging.

While passing is a slippery concept, it's a useful one to consider critically in any scenario where you might possess a strong desire to be treated or seen as someone who belongs but may feel – or may be encouraged by others to feel – that you don't. Regardless of the context and whether you do or do not objectively 'fit in' in a particular environment (though that idea itself seems quite reductive and subjective), a wish to 'pass' is something that can be a great source of stress and very injurious to a person's confidence. It comes ultimately from a fear of being 'found out'; of trying very hard to blend into a particular environment or community and falling short of the imposed standard of entry in some way.

I remember my English cousins, born to Irish parents, telling me they were Irish when they visited most summers during my childhood. They would make this declaration in the broad, flat clip of a London accent before trying to belt one another in the legs with a hurley they'd procured somewhere – a handy prop in the performance of Irish identity. I didn't understand how they could consider themselves to be what I was when it seemed so clear to me that they weren't. That their belonging was impossible. Their inauthentic performance struck me as such a failed attempt at passing that the clear effort it involved only exacerbated my contempt. I could feel how badly they wanted to own the identity, and even as a child the strength of the desire struck me as pathetic. Covetous, even. Deluded.

The fault was mine. I couldn't have adequately defined what being Irish meant if anyone had asked me. I was rejecting their statements based solely on how their claim to membership of what I saw as *my* in-group made me feel. Also kind of based on the hurley thing – that's truly unhinged behaviour. They didn't speak or dress like 'us', they didn't live among 'us', so they were not 'us'. They were 'them'. It seemed simple enough, but then I was about ten. Your powers of analytical sophistication are limited when you're ten. I can remember feeling almost angry with them – these alien invaders with their foreign voices and effortful performance of what I took for granted as my own – as though in claiming to be what I considered myself to be, they were trying to take something from me. As though Irishness is a finite resource and one to which I had some inherent right to stand as gatekeeper.

Though I didn't have the language for it then and the concept was much too challenging for a small child to navigate, I was grappling with the knowledge that my cousins didn't pass. Their outgroup accents, phrasing and interests all revealed them to be claiming an identity that they could not convincingly perform to members of the in-group. When they didn't understand the words and phrases we used, or spoke in their flat, foreign tones, it seemed clear to me that in saying they were Irish, they were really saying they would *like* to be Irish. I disliked them intensely for refusing to accept what I decided they were, and I thought no more deeply about it. Given that they arrived every summer with their parents and were allowed to stay up late and belt one another when provoked without consequences, I probably would have disliked them regardless. But statements about Irishness expressed in an accent the contemporary school curriculum suggested was that of descendants of heartless colonisers didn't help. Whatever I am, I thought, they surely cannot be.

*

Like any nation, Ireland is a set of ideas that expand or contract depending on how broadly you consider them. As a result of its disparate faces and concepts, many things have been named after Irish people and their ancestral homeland. There's Irish coffee (this is coffee, but for alcoholics or people who need something to settle their nerves after receiving an unexpected call telling them with spectacular frankness that a beloved relative is dead). An Irish goodbye (you don't strictly have to be Irish to engage in this one; you simply decide you've reached your emotional limit at a party but lack the social skills to articulate this, so you leave without telling anyone you're going so that people ask, 'Where's Dave?' or 'Where's Amy? The prick. Have they done it again?' after you've left). Also there are Irish twins (when a baby arrives within a year after its older sibling, to the presumed decimation of its mother's bone mass, sanity and disposable income).

There's Irish resistance. You finally manage to eject the British after a few hundred years of colonial rule, but only from twenty-six counties (awkward). You then develop a little-sister complex so all-encompassing that you're still cutting in a DIY fringe behind the locked bathroom door in a self-annihilating attempt to look more like big sister over a hundred years after she's left home and mostly forgotten you exist. A lot of the things named for us are really rather insulting when you think about it. These names extend Ireland and its people the sort of low-expectation-induced (albeit fond) licence you might give to a relative who attends your wedding with his trousers on backwards but whose good sense of humour really cannot be argued with. Yet, we remain an affable people. For the most part. To your face, anyway.

We'll welcome any visitor in theory but we'll talk about them like there's something truly amiss if they elect to stay. Not to mention the fact that they'll still be whisperingly denigrated as a 'blow-in' behind stiff hands at their Irish funeral seven decades later. As though their trustworthiness with the key to the silver cabinet remains under review till further notice. We'll also condemn anyone who leaves, so there is that too. This condemnation will reverberate with overtones of 'who do they think they are?' To leave is to desire something else, and to experience desire is to be unhappy with what you have now. To be unhappy with what you have now is to presume you deserve better. If you've been to Ireland at all, you'll know that general consensus has determined that you don't.

Irish people grow up apologising for themselves. Consequently, we police the behaviour of one another jealously. It is a sort of cultural hangover and inheritance. An intergenerational imperative. Not all people who feel shame are Irish, but all Irish people feel shame much or most of the time. It is knitted into and through the skeleton of our culture – not the one internationally associated with Ireland, the merrymaking, ah-sure-come-on-inning, arbitrarily poetic and wryly humorous salt-of-the-earth culture, but the real thing. The harder thing from which all the fluffier stuff emerges. The bread and butter of Irish everydayness.

The culture that Irish people actually grow up in and live in. The one keeping our spines straight enough to hold us upright. The one that teaches fitting in as the cardinal virtue and drawing attention to yourself (inadvertently or otherwise) as *the* cardinal sin.

Shame is a principal Irish pastime, along with coming from a family of older women who won't stop overfeeding everyone carbohydrates and then accuse them of having 'gone very fat altogether'. It's a national pastime, like Gaelic football or hurling. Not a professional sport, but something in which people participate with a level of commitment that makes it seem they must surely be paid for their labour. Shame is our meat and potatoes. The amniotic fluid within which we sprout limbs and creak into being. It has arisen and endured through centuries of colonialism, Catholicism and a confusing ideological soup of liberalism floating conspicuously atop enduring small-'c' conservatism. What is shame really but the consciousness of oneself conceived in the awareness of the other? Reflected smallness, or the anticipation of it. The country with a gnawing cognisance of its small size in a political landscape of bigger players, Ireland is classically post-colonial – simultaneously dismissive of and obsessed by its status and reputation in the eye of the 'other'.

Before leaving London for Australia, I went home to Ireland for three months after six years of living in the UK. Home to Limerick. The small south-western city that feels like a town no matter where you're standing. Like most places with a history of being forgotten, minimised or considered the butt of a joke by the rest of the country, Limerick prompts in its residents both a sense of defensiveness and an urge to mitigate its reputation combined with grumbling among themselves that the place is inherently dreadful and things will obviously never get better. From my earliest realisation that there were other places in the world where a person might live, I nurtured a violent desire to leave Limerick.

The city seemed to me perpetually grey and perpetually damp, a uniquely gloomy point on the earth's latitude. As though you might almost reach up and touch the sodden clouds dumped like dirty towels onto a glass ceiling that lay, oppressively, just feet above your head. It felt as though you conducted your days in a crouch. It is a place where to this day there endures a restaurant called Stuffin's Chinese and European Cuisine. It has stood across the street from Limerick's St Joseph's psychiatric hospital and the city's prison for thirty years and is painted a raging shade of penitentiary orange so that it comes at you fast as you approach regardless of the speed you're moving at. The visual of this trifecta as you'd pass by in a car (it isn't a scenic spot to linger in) struck my adolescent brain as encapsulating the inherent strangeness and absurdity of my home town. A combination of the desolate and the surreal that somehow landed with humour. The place where someone will walk up to you and say 'C'mere and I tell you a question' or 'You're a pure gowl, you are' and if you're not from the city you consult your knowledge of how the English language works, only to presume based on the evidence that you're probably having a stroke and your brain is processing the words in the wrong order.

During our months at home, I brought my English husband into a butcher's shop on Limerick's William Street, where he pointed to some mince and politely asked, 'Is this beef?' The butcher replied, 'It would be, yeah.' A vast pause ensued during which the butcher eventually looked at me with an expression of severe judgement for having brought an uncomprehending twit into his shop. J. could not understand what was happening, grammatically or otherwise. Was it theoretical beef? Conditional beef? Hypothetical beef? Was the butcher suggesting there are conditions under which this minced meat was not now but might somehow become beef? After a baffled exchange between the two, which was conducted in English but not a shared version, I told J. that yes, this is in fact beef and that here and in other parts of the country, to say something 'would be' in certain contexts is the same as to say 'it is'. He bought some beef mince, possibly out of embarrassment. On the walk home I had to explain the linguistic particularities to him, and how 'would be' emerges from the Irish-language descriptions of the habitual present tense. Like other places in Ireland, Limerick has its own lexicon, tone and iteration of Hiberno-English. It is a place where reality often feels inverted and things which seem familiar can be rendered anything but. A place where context is supreme and the world as you know it can slant and slide. Where beef can be conditional or transform into something else.

I watched *Angela's Ashes* in my early teens, observed its depiction of the Limerick city of the 1940s and 50s as an economically deprived, rain-soaked hellscape – a representation which enraged and offended countless Limerick people on the release of the film, directed by Alan Parker and based on the Pulitzer Prize-winning memoir by Frank McCourt – and thought, *Well, yeah. They've caught the mood of the place anyway.* Of course, I had to grow up and be kicked about a bit by other places to recognise that my loathing of my home town was more about me than the place itself. That, and the slums of McCourt's Limerick had long been demolished. Also, we had an H&M so it's not quite the same. I was just being an arse.

Stuffin's restaurant or no, Limerick is certainly one of the strangest places I've ever set foot in. The sense of ossification that characterised the city of my youth, as though the place itself and my life there were suspended in aspic, was dashed asunder and rendered far less unappealing by the sort of adulthood I never quite anticipated – one of constant change, emigration and ultimately the loss of the home in Limerick, which I had spent my childhood taking for granted, when my mother died when I was in my twenties. Our house was sold when she became too sick to work, taking my sense of place with it. She died shortly after, taking with her most of my sense of self and my primary connection to home.

After that, Limerick was too difficult a place to be in. Simultaneously unchanged and unrecognisable, like the morning after the end of the world. My mother had been the fulcrum of my life there. Suddenly it was not the adolescent trap it had previously felt like but a sepulchre – everything from the capricious Shannon river to the famed curse of St Munchin, which decreed that no person from Limerick will flourish in their native city. An inside joke. The place where 'would be' means 'is'. Representations of representations. Something transformed beyond recognition so that everything familiar felt alien. Home had been a person more than a place, or perhaps the person and place had become synonymous without my realising it. Now, the schism broke all of it. London followed Dublin, and seven different homes in eight years.

There was a barn in the West Midlands of the UK for eleven months, where I largely stayed indoors developing a vitamin D deficiency that made my body the enemy of my mind. Apart from waking with the shrieking wrench of leg cramps in the middle of the night (the signals intelligence of a poorly nourished and neglected body) I was preoccupied by the business of despairing under the shifting burdens of grief, a completely unrecognisable life, and a looming PhD deadline for a doctorate I was then completing in large part to assuage the ambitions of my recently dead mother. The barn sat in a barnyard in the middle of a stretch of unrelentingly damp, languid English countryside that struck me as profoundly desolate in the cramped corridor of a bleak British winter. Next door lived a deaf, geriatric terrier named Biscuit (because he couldn't hear his own bark, you could hear his bark from space). Across the yard lived a red-trouser-clad Tory of the bloviating old school 'in my day men were men and the working class worked' type. I don't mind Tories one bit. Politics are fine. It's red trousers that are objectionable – it is a touch unimaginative to wake in the morning and choose to live one's life as a P.G. Wodehouse character, only without the irony. Or the humour.

This neighbour barked out every statement (the man, though also Biscuit) with the tone of someone holding up a bank with a sawn-off shotgun or verbally directing a local peasant into an oubliette for inadvertently lingering briefly on the wrong side of a fence. Each utterance was gifted to the world as a form of declarative fact which it did not seem to occur to him that anyone might dispute. He called over during working hours one chilly December afternoon, as a retired neighbour does, to observe that our Christmas tree was particularly small and to remark that as a rule he didn't visit provincial parts of the UK like Liverpool or Ireland.

I had the joy of seeing Leonard Cohen perform during his penultimate tour – he looked indulgently at his keyboard while it played its famous rudimentary auto-accompaniment to 'Tower of Song' and apologetically intoned 'it goes by itself' while the thrilled crowd laughed. This neighbour was similar to that keyboard. He went by himself. I endured the interaction by nodding silently with a solemn expression while imagining him being bundled into a cannon and shot directly into the surface of the sun. Sometimes you make the effort to engage and sometimes you keep your peace and watch objects retreat into the distance. Whatever gets you to the other side.

We lasted eleven months in Warwickshire before grief rendered me unrecognisable to myself and I tired of the inane mimicry of my accent that occurred every time I ventured into the local town. Limerick may have felt like a shirt that didn't fit but it turned out the English countryside suited no better. It was there that I realised Irishness is a thing that only happens to you after you leave home.

Irishness is a coat you cannot remove. There are other coats, which are harder to wear. Still, we're all closest to the coat on our own back. National identity is one of the lenses through which others filter us. The impression such a coat creates is inescapable. Sometimes you sweat beneath its heat and bulk, or it itches or pinches under the armpits so that it feels as if your arms are always held in front of you, unbent in protective supplication. 'Please,' they suggest, '. . . enough.'

That coat doesn't feel directly relevant to most situations in which you find yourself and yet on you must trundle, wearing it. And so it is made relevant by those around you, often and especially in those moments when you manage briefly to forget that you're wearing it at all. It's shrugged on in the airport departures lounge and you sweat in it as an emigrant until you come home again to the place where Irishness is less relevant and obvious merely because it is a cluster of vague concepts that exist in almost everyone around you. In Ireland, Irishness is not encapsulated or represented by any one individual but the by suspension in which we all float. For those within the in-group, it can be a means of easy and immediate connection rather than distance. A shared starting point. A cultural commonality, though coming home can generate its own problems. This was true for me even when my mother was alive.

Visits home were conducted with intense trepidation. Just as returning to your parents' house might cause you to revert to a petulant, ungenerous, huffing adolescent even though you're thirty-five now and have house insurance and a certificate from that adult scuba-diving course you did that one time, going back to your childhood home can effect pretty much the same catastrophic and embarrassing psychological devolution. You reprise the role of 'you, but ten/fifteen/twenty years ago', become fifteen again and settle in around the entrenched expectations of everyone involved, including yourself. The shift in gears is so natural you only notice once it has already occurred, observing that you've somehow become the most uncharitable, judgemental and impatient version of yourself. A version you remember well and intensely dislike, sluicing forth a fetid bilge of sullen resentment toward those who remind you that the adolescent twat is still very much in there, pouting greasily close to the surface.

Until we returned for a protracted stay before leaving for Australia, the odd week-long visit here and there had been the extent of my direct interaction with home. Just enough to prevent any meaningful immersion and insulate the life I had painstakingly built from the one I had escaped. Of course, after a brush with madness when I was twenty, I returned to Limerick for a year to work in a bookshop and seek out the shards of my sanity, but that was different. My mother was still alive then and home was an intact, unimpeachable concept. Apart from that year of great unravelling, when antidepressants and madness would wake me nightly in a lagoon of glacial sweat and broiling fear, a couple of days never felt long enough to accidentally glance my former self on the city streets the way I would see people I once went to school with, or worked retail or factory jobs with, or who lived on my street. Faces sighing past like the rows of cans in Elizabeth Bishop's poem 'The Filling Station'. Streaking by blurrily in the interrogative 'ssso? sso? so?' of hissing streetlamps as you move on by in the seat of a car. I would try not to stay long enough to be pulled back into a past that bit at my heels as I ran from it all through my twenties. Or to have to consider that just as my mother had been Limerick and so Limerick was home, part of her inheres in it still, and so it was, is, would ever be. It took a long time to accept that we never really leave the place we come from. It is a gift and a curse, giving rise to the stories we build around who we are.

After my mother died, I rarely returned. Until I knew that Australia would place a distance between me and the town I grew up in, which, in typical, clichéd fashion, rendered me more appreciative of it. Less afraid. In fairness, five years in the petrified, labyrinthine class maze that is London media circles was sufficient softening-up to teach me appreciation for my origins. For a place whose wavelength I understood without having to climb onto or duck crabwise under it. Not to mention the intractable fact of those origins. When you gain access to the rooms you can only imagine as an Irish kid with limited prospects, you quickly realise that others will neither overlook nor forget where you come from, regardless of how comfortably – or otherwise – you own it. You're wearing the coat whether you want to or not. The choice you have is how to wear it.

When my mother was alive I would go home to Limerick with the mentality of the eighteen-year-old girl who left it the instant she could (minus the bad haircut and the firm belief that 'nobody gets me'), ready to run up the stairs and slam my bedroom door after I generate the hostile conditions that ensure nobody does indeed 'get me'. Or maybe they do because I'm being an arse and that's pretty straightforward. This time, despite being incontrovertibly deep into adulthood, still I came prepared to be huffy and aloof despite the fact that Limerick was different and so was I. I was prepared to reprise the role of my least evolved self. Ready to feel adolescent, alien and conspicuous. Ready to be eyeballed for a weird garment. Weird being anything that isn't collectively endorsed as standard (and therefore indicates the possible presence of subversiveness – also understood as Britishness). Or judged to have 'notions' for living a life that is untypical – also considered a rejection – of where I grew up.

Notions are the vague but terrible sin of seeking to break with conformity in an Irish context. Of being seen to presume oneself elevated or better by deviating from the norm. It is a funny phrase couched in culturally enforced Irish humour and humility, but it also reveals a dark collective assumption – that a person should ultimately be what we expect them to be. Even after all this time there was plenty to go on in the notions stakes as I anticipated several months back at home, despite the fact that my mother had been gone for years. The writing. The notions London aesthetic. The childlessness. The black husband with a British accent.

In Limerick, my paternal grandmother used to greet someone new by peering at them as though they might be trying to conceal a criminal record, then asking, 'And who are your people?' As though the two of them were already deep in a conversation and all the pleasantries demanded by basic etiquette had been dispensed with. And why not? She was operating on the belief that, in some respect, you were already acquainted. It was Limerick, so you probably were. If she didn't know you, she knew someone you were related to or otherwise closely connected with. She knew your people.

This is a hilarious and mildly embarrassing feature of Irishness more generally. One Irish person can meet another for the first time in Australia or Singapore or the US and discover that their brother's best friend's cousin plays hurling with the other Irish person's aunt's podiatrist. It's not a big country. Here in Australia, my husband met an Irish woman through his job whose husband, it turns out, grew up down the street from me. I am currently sitting at a desk located over seventeen thousand kilometres away from Limerick and outside are skeletal, ink-black crickets the length of house keys singing as though it will save them, but the distance is nothing. That's just how Irishness works.

When my English mother-in-law – an East Londoner – asked me, with a face as serious as a tax return, whether I know everyone who lives in Dublin, I was tempted to spiral into the classic 'eight hundred years of oppression' speech that Irish people save for these sorts of occasions. It's an offensive question and presumes a provincialism which, while impossible in the literal sense, gestures (here, with a classically British colonial complacency) at a connectivity widely understood to be a feature of Irishness. 'No,' I answered flatly. 'I don't personally know two million people,' wondering for a second whether that was, in fact, true. Because in fairness to my mother-in-law, Irish people do somehow tend to find one another all over the world.

I envisioned her mental image of my country's capital city as a cookfire-scented wattle-and-daub village or some sort of British outpost turned savage. Dublin has a Pret now, allowing me to recreate the precise feeling and flavour (burnt coffee beans smelling of a rarely cleaned machine) which evokes commuting in and out of London from its suburbs every day and then hunching beneath the queasy fluorescent strip lighting in one or other of its partially empty post-pandemic communal office spaces (where inevitably someone asks me if I know everyone in Dublin).

Yet it's not all that far off the presumption underlying my grandmother's question. *And who are your people?* In her Limerick – the one she was born into, grew up and grew old in – a person's reputation was solidified in this way, so that they might be understood through the lens of the family or community from which they emerged. There is something lovely in this – the idea that you are not considered an isolated entity but as a fragment of a whole. A greater entity. As though you are one point within a temporal and causal chain. A single unit rooted within a wider network and therefore to some extent both inherently insulated and understood. You exist within a context of shared values, history and culture. Within a shared, co-constituted story. This can be nourishing and deeply reassuring; these parts of ourselves we share with those around us and therefore don't have to explain, justify or defend. It is why national identity is comforting among people who share this context but becomes the coat you cannot take off among others.

Yet there is also something akin to strangulation in being viewed primarily through this communal lens, even at home. It guarantees that the sins of your kin become yours to carry and your individual potential is decided in reference to those who preceded you. In my own case, that feels like a pretty raw deal. The pattern of your internal and external life is determined by reference to family, culture and the limits of the imagination of the people in your orbit. We have necessary obligations to family and to community. Yet when they encroach on us in ways that seek to limit our capacity to develop elements of identity which may clash with the ones we have inherited, problems arise. There is not much room within that context for telling a new story.

In this way, the question – *And who are your people?* – is not just an enquiry about your unique cultural and chronological context but the opening volley in an evaluation that is not really about *you* at all, or not in an exhaustive sense. *Come here and tell me who you come from so that I can tell you who you are.* The problem arises when this evaluation claims – as it often does – to encapsulate us in our entirety. It is not *who* we are but a mere part, and that part is descriptive rather than prescriptive. It describes the past but not necessarily the present or future, and this is something that is too often overlooked or forgotten.

Americans are better at individual identity than Irish people are. Notwithstanding the problems that arise when the concept of the individual is elevated to the point of solipsism, their culture sits atop a foundation of ideas like natural rights and individual liberty. When you come from a place whose culture (again, at least in theory) celebrates a person's right to live as they see fit provided they don't impede the ability of others to do the same, claiming and occupying your own individuality is a relatively uncontroversial and even admirable thing to do. In cultures like ours on this side of the Atlantic, particularly in the context of Ireland, whose colonisation necessitated the formation of a collective identity rooted in part in 'notness', the individual has historically been discouraged as a mode of self-identification.

When a culture or community moves to collectivise in opposition to a threat and an imposed identity – which many Irish people did for centuries – it is not useful to encourage individuals to wander off in their own direction and 'find themselves'. Irish parents would simply respond, 'Sure you're just there in front of me. I can see you, like. What's there to be finding?' Under threat conditions, to be casual about identity is to cede ground to the 'other' side. To generate ambiguity on which the other might capitalise. More than that, it is to allow a perceived outsider to determine identity for you. When there is a point to prove or an oppressor to whoosh off your front lawn through a combination of guerrilla warfare and some other, grittier means, there is not the luxury of fostering individual identity. Where there is not collective self-determination, there can never be individual self-determination.

Of course, there are costs to promoting individuality – loss of social cohesion and collective meaning among others. They aren't minor problems and appear to some degree in every secularised Western country. The friction between our desire for uniqueness and our tendency to seek validation of our self-image from groups is at the heart of the modern identity crisis. But then, everything has its costs.

Collectivisation, and consequently conformity, might be considered necessities under such circumstances. Jump ahead eighty or a hundred years from the formation of the Irish state and you have a country where you may be frowned upon for such deluded actions as once having worn a biker jacket to your brother's birthday party in a local pub (only to be referred to as 'Danny Zuko' in the local town for the ensuing thirty years) or articulating anything implying self-esteem or non-conformity in front of other people. To dissent, or rather not to conform, is tacitly digested and understood within the culture as a rejection of the Irish social and political project. It is a threat to the ideas that founded a nation's self-image through collective energy and collective opposition. So it's a joke that you're Danny Zuko because you wore the leather jacket once, but also it isn't. And it's a bit of fun, but also it is a socially endorsed punitive intervention. A course correction. We have developed an association between conformity and trustworthiness. Between familiarity and humility. Between shame and Irishness.

When I had just got the news of my place at university to study philosophy and English literature, my mother shared the news with her visiting friends, a married couple, while blooming with pride. Visits were rare in our family, and so was any of us gaining entry to Trinity College, so my mother was having a good day. Her so-often anxious face unbolted and softened into a rare smile of legitimate happiness. The sort of smile that renders any face it moves over instantly beautiful. A smile that travels.

Her friend's husband witnessed this rare, unfurling radiance and said to me dourly, 'Ah, you'll be an English teacher so, will you?' The question was uttered without any upward inflection to differentiate it from a statement. 'I don't think so, no,' I answered, eighteen and baffled. 'I haven't made up my mind about what I'd like to do after university, really. I'm just really glad I got my place.' In the Limerick of the early 2000s, where there was no Frank McCourt slum but there was a museum exhibiting a mummified cat that someone found on Nicholas Street in the 1890s, this deeply conceited reply was naturally considered the verbal equivalent of whipping a flick knife out of my sock and threatening to orphan the man's children.

He audibly scoffed, a piece of masticated scone flying forth from his mouth, which had unhinged itself slightly in an irksome combination of complacency and shock. 'But *of course* you'll be a teacher.' The unspoken end of the sentence was '*you flighty, arrogant little nitwit.*' He looked at me with enough weariness to melt the face from a department store mannequin and his voice rattled with patronising certainty. 'Sure, that's all you can do with *that* degree.'

There it was. In that moment, the world was a box of his creation, and his father's before him, and we all had a fixed place in it. We all had our galvanised point soldered into the network. It was seen as a heinous act of self-aggrandisement to study anything so willowy and impractical (fair enough), but then on top of this, to presume I might be able to create any options for myself outside the path he saw ahead of me. The one that lay ready to walk down. The one determined by consensus.

'Who do you think you are?' is a common reaction in Ireland. You'll find it in raised eyebrows and the comments sections under influencers' social media posts. In Reddit discussions and conversations between friends as they discuss anyone from political leaders to TV personalities to the overdressed woman at the supermarket. It views non-conformity or any aberration from established norms as a form of entitlement.

That word might still be reclaimed. Surely it is right and proper (when you are lucky enough to live in a place where you won't be imprisoned for non-conformity) to exercise that freedom, that entitlement. To wear the stupid leather jacket rather than see it hanging in your wardrobe every time you open the door and feel both resentful and weak when you choose not to wear it. Until the day you open the wardrobe and find that you too have decided the jacket is ridiculous. Surely it is better to see options for yourself, or to nurture the hope that you might work to create some, even if someone else's vision of your value and capability is fixed and confident. It is better to know that you are more than those around you decide you are. Or to behave as though that is true in the belief that it may become so.

We are alone inside ourselves every time we open the wardrobe door. We live alone inside our heads. We can share our lives with others but we are limited by and answerable only to ourselves when determining the elements of identity that help comprise who we are. We can participate in the stories people tell us about ourselves, but we don't have to. We can feel entitled to go another way, to try things, to fail without reference to other people's decision that a failure constitutes the end of a story rather than the beginning or middle of one. There are malignant forms of entitlement, but some forms are simply articulations of self-possession. In Irish culture, we have no healthy sense of the difference between the two.

You could build a sturdy argument on the idea that perpetually feeling like a failure is simply the resting psychological state of any individual who has emerged as intended from an Irish upbringing and education. You wouldn't be far off the mark if you did. Confidence was powerfully and overtly discouraged by the polyester-skirt-and-sensible-shoe-clad nuns whose stern and discouraging expressions punctuated my school years.

Had there been a mantra overtly spoken rather than merely reinforced through environment, culture and values it would have been something along the lines of 'Aim for the mean, but no further.' There was no greater guarantee of ostracism than meaningful ambition, an inclination toward individuality, or resistance to conformity. Ambition was fine, provided you aimed for something considered both valuable and adequately humble within the context of the culture. But the kind of ambition that inclined you to wonder whether a space might be carved into the world to fit you rather than contorting yourself into the space that was waiting? No. Not that. Never that. You are not entitled to try to traverse the world in irregular ways, to question norms or to value creativity, which is of course a fundamentally subversive activity and attitude. Difference was – and to some extent still is – considered a threat to homogeneity. This is because it *is* a threat. It always has been.

Irish culture and our historical narrative are relatively quiet on the many Irish people who happily identified as British at various points in our country's history. We don't talk much about those who did not support our country's independence. They blur the preferred story, which generally tilts its head to the side, squints and retroactively presumes that there was a universal desire for Irish independence, or that ill will toward the people whose ancestors rocked up and booted ours off their patch of land seethed in the breast of every 'true' Irish person. Or – more gasp-inducing still – those who thought colonisation had brought some benefits or that some active participation in the Anglosphere (however it was initiated and despite the bigotry and injustice that certainly came with it) was preferable to the alternative, which was unlikely to be an isolationist Celtic utopia.

Those people were understandably considered a deeper threat to emerging conceptions of independent Irish identity even than the British themselves, in whose interest it was that no such conception of Irishness should coalesce within the context of a country that the world (and some of Ireland itself) considered British. Emerging from a history of such competing conceptions of what it means and meant to be Irish, we have learned to impose strict barriers to entry and familiarised ourselves with the idea that a person's Irishness is decided largely by committee. It is determined by what the collective perceives a person *not* to be rather than how an individual positively identifies themselves. My cousins with their hurley and their London accents come to mind.

For these and other reasons, Irishness has developed into something one does not – cannot – opt into or out of, despite our passport becoming so coveted post-Brexit. Throughout history it has variously been a secret or forbidden identity, a label of prejudice, a means of ostracism, a source of pride, a proxy for religious affiliation, the butt of a joke, a closely guarded in-group signifier, an insulting way of exiting a party, a spiked coffee and a coat that you cannot take off. Whatever Irishness is, it isn't one thing alone. And like many other identity labels people consider self-evident, it is as opaque and murky as the Chicago river dyed a livid green for St Patrick's Day. A pastiche of Irishness that transforms it into something else. A representation of a representation. A baffling intertextual reference that is so far from its already nebulous origins as to raise more questions than it could ever presume to answer. But even a green river is someone's version of Irishness in a world where identity is more multifaceted and less homogenous than ever before. Where people are allowed to be more than just one thing, Irishness is necessarily also more than one thing.

That Irish identity as it has evolved in recent history and formed in the seething heat of opposition is not all bad – there is pride and community and a collective understanding that culture erodes without active participation and devoted appreciation. We have an enormously enthusiastic and loyal diaspora – one that Irish people tend not to appreciate even if the Irish government understands how critical that diaspora is, both economically and culturally.

Neither, however, is an identity formed in defensive anger completely positive. Nothing which comes into being in reaction to something it hates and seeks to minimise within its cultural legacy can be entirely constructive. It must contain its punitive and coercive elements. To be Irish is in part to be 'not British'. Colonised places are eternally marked by their colonisation and are consequently unable to access their identity in isolation from their colonial history and experience. Such an identity no longer exists but they must maintain the illusion of an essential, untouched, or 'pure' national identity to have something left upon which to build and reinforce identity once the grabby lads are booted out.

Such cultures – such countries as Ireland – are seemingly left with no option but to fill the breach by forming their identity in direct reference and opposition to their colonisers. In the reactivity of remaking itself after British occupation (and the hegemonic cultural oversight of the Catholic Church), some part of Irishness inheres in resentment of other and defensiveness of self. When Ireland finally managed to get a big enough stick under the British and winkle them out, the place and people were changed – part of the intertextual legacy of Irishness, which has adapted and blended around and through its history. There was no return to a then-lost identity. What we 'were not' was a decent enough proxy for identity to fill the gaps in what we were. When Irish people did form a nation state of their own, part of our 'not-Britishness' inhered in Catholicism. It was one of the elements that qualified Irish people as not British and therefore as Irish. For decades, Irish people overlooked the fact that we had largely replaced one hierarchical power with another. Without a sound sense of collective and national identity as distinct from conflict and the moral and functional guidance of external oversight, we had in large part given away a sovereignty that we either didn't recognise or didn't quite know how to manage.

Call it trauma, but that word is grievously overused and more often than not seems applied by bad actors in justification of poor behaviour rather than used as a value-neutral descriptor for the benefit of people who have been profoundly harmed and seek a constructive way through the dark legacy this harm thrust upon them. In the lazier, more common contemporary usage, the word 'trauma' is a skeleton key. It justifies rather than explains, and it implies no fault. There is fault in this case. There is an ugliness and a smallness in Irish culture for which we are now responsible – we've been in charge for a while, after all. So our faults must be both our burden and our property. We still guard jealously as though in affirming who we are not, and who doesn't belong, we might reify who we are.

5

Race

Le bonheur écrit à l'encre blanche sur des pages blanches
('Happiness writes in white ink on white pages')
– Henry de Montherlant

IN THE HOSPICE, LAUGHTER always feels subversive.
As though death is a purely solemn business, imper-
meable to the absurd, the mundane or the silly. It's
true that she has come to the hospice to die but that
isn't a constant topic of conversation between us. Being
alive is so often both silly and mundane. These elements
encroach frequently and with little respect on the
process of dying. As long as she is living, there are
mundane and silly things to consider. The chicken at
lunch arrives with a volume of gravy on it that evokes
a particularly unappetising soup. Someone compli-
ments her purple pyjamas. People visit and they say
things they don't mean because they don't know how
to find the truth when every conversation could be the
last one. At this moment, she is still living. Rendered

functional through the palliative relief granted by liberal doses of methadone.

Until I saw a nurse bustle into the room merrily, in that bustling, nursey way – with an air that is part motherhood, part militarism – and hand the drug to her for the first time, I had only ever been aware of it as a transitional alternative for heroin addicts. I hadn't realised that methadone is a liquid dosed out into a tiny plastic cup and swallowed as a child might swallow a spoon of Calpol. Methadone – a synthetic opioid that can mitigate a terminal cancer patient's pain without giving them the euphoric high associated with other opioids – is absinthe green. It looks preposterously like a cartoon medicament. Like some sort of prop in a TV movie. In this instance, its action is to sever the connection between the voracious cancer thoughtlessly devouring its way through my mother's shrinking body and her brain's ability to register the terrible pain of that rigorous, barbarous process. Methadone is used in palliative care, I later learned, because it is potent, long-lasting and cheaper than many alternatives. A livid-green solution to more than one devastating problem.

She is laughing at J. My first actual real-life 'in it for the long haul' boyfriend, despite the mildly humiliating fact that I am twenty-six. The initial months of our relationship should ideally have been, like all new relationships, a process of falling in love with the partial reflection of oneself cast in the eye of another person.

Populating the new space created by an as-yet largely unknown individual with the best-case scenario. A narcotic turmoil of uncertainty, yearning and release as two young people tumble together into a myopic vortex of new desire for one another, marvelling at the miraculous reciprocity of their mutual enthusiasm with a cloying combination of timidity, triumph and arrogance, as though no one has ever experienced anything like this before. That's early love, and that's how it goes, but it was cut short the day a doctor sat my mother and me in a couple of livid orange plastic chairs in a drab little room and told us in a tone of mild disinterest that she had terminal pancreatic cancer. The room had those austere, narrow windows that loom just below the ceiling. Like a bathroom in a service station or a middling basement restaurant. The kind of room where people go to do things unobserved and the architecture emphasises that escape is discouraged.

Four months later, we are sitting together in her hospice room. She is leaning against the pillows and laughing at J. At six foot five, he is conspicuous and exceptionally uncoordinated. A dapper-looking young man with neat, curly black hair, he's wearing a waxed Barbour jacket and cannot walk in a straight line while holding two cups of tea without spilling them in juddering, almost theatrical jerks onto the floor. He gifts most of the tea to the linoleum as he minces through the entryway, smiling apologetically as though he's conscious of breaching the solemn dignity of the hospice by making a scene like this. I rise silently, smiling, and wipe the floor while he puts the tea down with methodical deliberation. Because it's something to focus on and because he must not know what to think, this vital young man who I have pulled from the energy of early courtship and into this building where people come to die.

We have had to emerge from the lurid intensity of newly kindled desire and the youthful fervour of passionate intellectual connection to navigate the prag-matic world. I have discovered that it is a world where people you love and need can die slowly yet rapidly before your eyes in a few short months. Where the tiny bean of a camouflaged gland encamped in a person's guts can take silently against them inside the dark machine of their body. Where your sense of utter terror and despair become something from which you must protect your parent as a supreme act of love. Where, if you are a young man who has found himself suddenly deep within someone else's family crisis, your relationship with your new girlfriend quickly shifts from the novel electricity of new intimacy to getting on your knees to help wipe urine-hued tea from the floor of a room that countless lives have ended in, or holding her in the echoing mausoleum of a sleepless night while she weeps and talks incoherently about the uncanny colour of methadone.

My mother chuckles at the absurdity of such incom-petence in so large a person. J. is unaware that while

158

he was out of the room in search of ferrous-tasting tea, Emma – my mother, whom I had called by her name since I was an insufferable teenager – told me that really I should probably go on ahead and marry him. 'If you wanted to,' she says, as though it's just occurred to her that I might feel pressured otherwise given the gravity of the context. That if she didn't make this addendum the suggestion might take on the incontrovertible, leaden weight of a dying wish. That it might land with hooked talons upon my unravelling life like a pterodactyl or an edict. She isn't the kind of mother who goes about just telling you to marry people. Her statement is proof of the dire conditions under which we all now find ourselves. It feels reactive, like an attempt to carve order out of chaos with whatever tools happen to be to hand. Like an attempt to assemble something new as the life we've had together falls apart.

Since I was old enough to stand up on cobby legs and waddle about after my older brother, this woman has taught me that there are very few problems I would ever have to which a man might represent a feasible solution. 'There will be times when you will find yourself on your own in this life. So you have to know how to help yourself. You might be the only one who can,' she'd say, endlessly. Do I know how to help myself? I have always relied on her help. All her sentiments of splendid isolation are trickling away now as she seeks the comfort of knowing I won't be totally alone without her. I don't blame her but it's not a good reason to marry someone I have been in a relationship with for a little over a year. 'Some day, perhaps,' I tell her gently, doing the only thing I know how to do – the only thing she taught me to do in these situations – and giving her an undesirable truth instead of a comforting story. 'But not any time soon. This isn't a good time for big decisions.'

J. had won her over despite her unflinching certainty that she would dislike him. We had been a closed unit of three – Emma, my brother and me. This was a scenario borne first of necessity and then of habit. More than a year earlier, I had sat at the dinner table at home as usual, fresh off the Dublin train for a visit, only this time I had change to presage with her. Of course, by then she was already ill but we didn't know that yet. She had been different for a while – having digestive problems, seeming a little more emotional and a little less patient than usual, but then I had never brought a boy home before. I had never wanted to and hadn't yet met one who was a regular enough feature to justify the difficulty I knew she would experience in adapting to make space for him. She had never liked my brother's girlfriends, struggling to accept that those independent adults she had so eagerly sought to create would eventually inevitably exercise that independence. She wanted it and she was threatened by it.

A year before this moment in her hospice room, my mother asked me what J. was like – this man I deemed worthy of bringing home to meet her – and I wondered what to tell her first. The question was delivered under the pretence of an open mind but I could see the alarm climbing in her. Her hands came together on the surface of the table, bracing for impact, the knuckles pinched together. Blanched. I considered how best to lower a cat into a tepid bath for its own good and told her that J. was very tall. That's a difficult quality to find fault with. That, like me, he was raised by his mother and like me, he has one older sibling. Like me, he had had an absent father who could not seem to make room for him and like me, he was then doing a PhD at an institution where people raised by single mothers weren't exactly the norm. 'He's English,' I told her. 'He lives in the UK.'

She liked this; I could tell. Distance is good (it keeps boys away) and she always possessed an inaccurate belief that highly educated people are automatically sharper than less educated ones. Living her life largely in working-class circles, my mother didn't have enough experience of the ways that information and stupidity can coalesce within one person. I tell her that J. is clever and interesting, reliable and kind. He dresses far better than I do and goes to the gym a lot. I tell her that he is like no one I've met before and that I would like her to meet him. Only then, after sharing detail to sketch the outline of this promising young man I like so very much, do I mention that J. is a black man.

After a pause, I am not in the hospice room but back at that table looking at my mother, neither of us knowing that within two years of this moment, none of it would be here. The table we sit at. The room it stands in. My mother. All gone. 'He's black?' she repeats. 'Okay.' That is how she says it. There is a tone of mild inquiry. Seeking clarification. It is not laden or loaded. It's just a question, as though I might mean anything at all by the statement or as though this is a test. She leaves it sitting on the tired pine table between us for me to peer at. The table I coloured at when I was four, my legs jutting straight out over the edge of the chair because they were too short to do anything else.

'So what does that mean?' I ponder this question that might be interpreted a thousand ways. Is it a question about skin tone, culture, values? Is it a question about J.'s identity as he sees himself, or my idea of who he is? Is it a material or an immaterial question, a reference to the fact that she doesn't really know any people who aren't white? It's 2014 and we are in Limerick. Whatever way I consider interpreting it, it seems that the question is not mine to answer. That it is not possible for me to answer. Ultimately, it is a question about J.'s identity.

*

I eventually did take Emma's advice and married him. It was good advice. These days, it is nine years since that day in her hospice room and only a little less since my mother's death. Since that time, conversations about race have become standard in many homes. The murder of George Floyd in Minneapolis in 2020 brought conversations about race to the fore in a way that felt, at the time, like it had all the raw energy of a locked door being kicked in. A reconstruction of our culture with all of the attendant chaos and collective rage inherent to the sort of rupture through which culture remakes itself.

My mother's small, difficult question – 'What does that mean?' – is one it seems the Western world has tried to grapple with since 2020. Writers like Thomas Chatterton Williams and Ireland's own Emma Dabiri have applied the question to considerations around whiteness, blackness and the ways in which we might challenge hard barriers between identity categories in order to feel more comfortable with the ambiguity and fluidity of race as a concept. How we might consider who is served by strict categories of racialised identity, and how we might challenge them while engaging with sensitivity in a world that remains obsessed with race. A world where identity labels – those we reject and those we claim – still matter.

J. and I talk about race a lot in our house, and identity more generally. It is a topic as open to rational exploration as any other. The frequency of our discussions is partially because a major theme of public discourse, over the last few years in particular, has been the role of collective identity in defining an individual one – the extent to which we are able (or it is ethical) to define ourselves outside our relationship to the groups we claim, or which claim us. Since we are all constantly in the process of making ourselves, there is a lot to discuss when the parameters within which it is considered acceptable to do that shift, which they undoubtedly have over the last fifteen years or so.

We live in a tolerance-obsessed time. I always think that tolerance is a grim ideal, and a particularly British one as the legacy of imperialism literally comes home to roost, since what is tolerance really but the ability to quietly endure something you dislike rather than actually finding the good in it? Congratulating oneself for forbearance. When was the last time you 'tolerated' something you consider inherently good or valuable? Tolerance is where desire meets reality and juts its jaw out. When the best we can seem to aim for is bearing the company of those who differ from us, one could argue that walls between identity groups have rarely felt more turgid and less flexible.

Race is also an unavoidable topic over our dinner table because there are a lot of identities jostling with one another under our roof, and this makes the identity discussion as inevitable as it is intellectually interesting – male, female, Irish, British, Jewish, white, black, autistic, and that's before you even get into the socio-economic, ideological or intellectual affiliations. The list is a rather long one, considering it applies to only two people finding so much in common across the distance of two lives and a table. It is also not exhaustive. Neither of us is captured within these labels. That is just a list, and a list is not a person. A person is not a list.

What first drew me to J., and continues to draw me to him, is his legitimate originality. I have never met anyone who is even remotely like him. Despite, or perhaps because of, the variety of occasionally anti-thetical identity groups to which his unusual ancestry and experience permit him to lay claim, he is defined entirely by none of them. Like all of us, he is more than the sum of his parts. Unlike all of us, he knows this, and lives accordingly.

Something wonderful happens when you love a person whose socially assigned collective identity – their ethnicity, religion, gender or some amalgamation of these three and more – is different from your own. I should be more precise – several wonderful things happen. One of them is the realisation that race is not the only relevant lens through which to filter your perspective of the other person and it is certainly not the primary one. Perhaps especially when it is the lens most rigidly imposed upon them by the world we live in. I can imagine some hackles raising reactively upon reading that. After all, how dare I – the white person in the relationship – say that? It is true, though. When you are in a loving relationship with a person whose ancestral origin is located in a different part of the world from yours, such that their skin tone or hair colour or texture, or some other physical feature is different, you don't engage with them through the lens of their immutable characteristics. There is only individual identity when you are together – that is the liberation of loving someone. You see them as an authentic and discrete entity in themselves, not an articulation or representation of a theoretical collective – you engage with them as an individual who is more than the sum of their parts.

Some people will conflate race with culture, presuming that a difference in one entails a difference the other, but I can find nothing in that apart from the baldest old-fashioned racism. This presumes a crude form of biological essentialism, suggesting that an African American from New York necessarily has something inherent or cultural in common with a person from Botswana, or that a Londoner of Asian ancestry necessarily shares some meaningful link or values with a woman going about her daily routine at home in the Japanese town of Shiranuka.

Of course, sometimes within an interracial relationship shared culture or values are insufficient to withstand the challenges of navigating the world together. Race is constantly relevant in your public life and this will find its way back home with you. Sometimes it can sour or destroy a relationship. There is discrimination, or stupid comments, or resentful looks. J. and I have had the withering glares, clicking tongues and drunken insults from people who look vaguely like one or other of us, and from people who don't. In the air hangs the sense that there are people who feel they can lay claim to either of us, or both, by making us the target of their disappointment, their expectation, or their ire. That there are people who can pass us on the street, cast a slow, saurian eye over the visual, and engage in an evaluation which they consider so valid and objective that they see fit to express it through the arrangement of their face or their language.

We live in a world which perceives colour blindness as an impossibility and interprets all claims to it as harmful. While no group is a monolith, only a lunatic or a fool would suggest that we currently live in a colour-blind world. While writers like Coleman Hughes espouse colour blindness as an ideal still very much worth pursuing, particularly in the context of the US, from whose particular African-American experience and history the concept evolved, while others maintain that it is a dangerous fiction, I am conscious that two realities can exist at once. The truth of a statement is not determined by the ethnicity of the individual expressing it, but I do think that some statements are more or less impactful depending upon who is speaking. Not all of us have lines in every play.

Yet in a romantic interracial relationship (or any close interpersonal bond based on love and respect), failing to prioritise race as an identity marker over others is not a refusal to acknowledge the other person's ethnicity, culture or relative difference in skin tone. It is not the pretence that the person you love is no different from you, nor a denial of their experience or of material reality. Neither is it ignorance of the other person's differing experience in a world which is, pragmatically speaking, very far from colour blind.

It isn't ignorance or insensitivity, or the fostering of an environment that inhibits anyone's ability to authentically express themselves. Rather, it is the understanding that you and the person you love are fundamentally the same sort of entity, joined by an emotional and intellectual commonality that must by its nature go deeper than the way the world perceives either of you. At home, you exist in a state beyond socially imposed identity. You are two individuals, together. Without the world peering in to tell you what you are, you are only what you perceive yourself to be. This is the identity we choose for ourselves. The one we inhabit without explanation or apology, and this version of us is the one that people who love us see. At home, there are – or should be – fewer coats we cannot take off.

Out in the world (which sometimes of course does encroach upon the privacy and peace of home) J. encounters challenges that I don't. I would have to be a fool or a bigot to deny it. I have witnessed people telling him that he 'isn't really black' when he's wearing a suit, and seen security guards follow him around shops when he's wearing a hoodie. He is regularly stopped at the self-service checkout in our local grocery store, his receipt checked and his bag of groceries inventoried against it. I go in there most days and have never once been stopped in this way. On his ordinary route through the world, J. is frequently underestimated, vilified, presumed to be more athletic than he is. His physical conspicuousness sets him apart. He is consistently viewed through a racial lens which superimposes assumptions about who he is and what he thinks. Assumptions about what he represents and believes, and how he might potentially behave.

I have witnessed him not-quite-welcomed as someone of mixed heritage in countless contexts. Over ten years I've watched other people view him through the construct of race and ignore every other element of his complex identity. All of the richness of his personhood, which of course entails Blackness but not Blackness alone. Together, we stand out. A visual contrast. Tall and dark hand in hand with short and pale. We stood out in Dublin, which is very white, and in Limerick, which is whiter. We stood out in London, though less so. In Australia, where the cultural and racial context is widely different but there is little understanding of Black culture as understood through an African-American or a Black British lens, we stand out more than ever before. J. consistently pays a higher cost for this than I do. He carries it. He is made to. All I can do is hold his hand. I can ensure that there is always someone beside him whose acceptance is not partial, conditional or confused. I can show him what I see when I look at him.

In his book *Knife: Meditations After an Attempted Murder*, Salman Rushdie writes that before the knife attack in which he was repeatedly stabbed and ultimately lost an eye as he began a lecture on writer safety in Chautauqua, New York in 2022, he had begun writing a story titled 'White Ink on a White Page'. He didn't finish the story but it features a protagonist called Henry, partially in reference to the famous quote from French writer Henry de Montherlant which opens this chapter. Rushdie writes: 'I wanted Henry to believe, Candide-fashion, that he lived in the best of all possible worlds. I thought, he can't possibly be a person of color if he's happy in that way. He had to be white.' In some sense, he is right. Reading about Rushdie's Henry, I thought of the warm, unwrinkled belonging that arises naturally from congruity. From belonging by default. Being part of and reflected by the majority, even in the barest cosmetic sense if not also deeper culturally resonant ones. The way that visual identity markers can lubricate our movement through our environment. How they can determine how much or how little we are obliged to carry into and through particular situations and contexts. Whiteness is certainly not a sufficient condition for the sort of congruity that may amount to the kind of happiness – that assumption of the default, that happiness which is contingent on belonging – represented by Rushdie's Henry, but it may be a necessary condition. At least in the places where J. and I have lived.

170

These days, there are more Irish people with skin tones that appear darker than the pale complexion I share with my Celtic ancestors. The most recent census data attests that about 1.5 per cent of the Irish population is Black. When I met J. a decade ago and we lived together in Dublin, it was even fewer. These Irish people play GAA, presumably for the same baffling lack of salary as everyone else. They too know what it is to stand at a Dublin bus stop in horizontal rain while the digital sign reads '9 minutes' for forty-five consecutive minutes, before completely disappearing (I'm referring to the bus rather than the sign announcing when the bus will come. Still, I wouldn't rule the latter out as an impossibility). They know the joys of a drunken (or sober) Tayto sandwich and the perpetual failings and posturings of various anaemic Irish governments. They know the poetry and the provincialism of our culture. More still, they know the social price of minority status in a way that most Irish people do not. What it is to be inside something and yet also to feel that there is a part of life that must always be lived as a person with their face pressed against the glass, looking in. This experience is J.'s experience too. To live in a place, be born in a place, be *of* a place and to be asked, as though a person is not themselves but a small, flickering bulb in a fixed network stretching backwards, 'Yes but where are you *really* from?'

While race and gender are the identity categories most acutely highlighted and currently discussed within our culture, there isn't one single identity marker that is a priori more important than any other within the context of any person's experience. We all express our individuality through concepts of collective identity, so there is a critical need for empathy in encountering the identity expression of other people. Philosophy and psychology have spent a sufficiently long time considering and looking for the 'self' – the idea of a fixed entity, bundle of concepts or behaviours that constitutes whatever 'I' am. Whatever 'you' are. Between the self we desire to be and the one we consider ourselves to be at any particular moment, the one we construct and signal in the external world and the one that others perceive through a combination of our signalling, the norms to which we are collectively subject and their own internal and external conception of 'self', it is impossible to find a single infallible objectivity. 'I' am not one thing but many things. Or rather more accurately, I am the thing that arises from a concatenation of many things.

When we lean too enthusiastically into a single identity marker, it becomes the lens through which we view not just ourselves but everyone else. It starts to dictate not only the limits of who and what we are but bleeds outward into our conception of other people. Other identities. We can begin to believe that we are the authority on how another person is allowed to identify, think or present themselves in the world. Our own identity can become so all-encompassing that it starts to assign motivations, beliefs and substance to others. Its forcefulness arises from its brittleness.

We are not obliged to see a person through the precise lens via which they view themselves but nor are we bolstering or protecting our own identity by dismissing someone else's as they see it. I identify as Irish – if you do too, then there may be some grounds for commonality between us, or at least enough conversation fodder to pass the time at a conference coffee break with some mutually polite conversation. If you consider yourself French, then perhaps we might discuss elements of our two respective cultures and connect that way.

What I'm not going to do is seek out the fact of the matter as though such concepts are empirical when they are not. I'm not going to ask to see your passport or your birth certificate, as though your sense of national identity is simply a matter of paperwork filed with the state. I'm not going to ask you to pronounce difficult place names like 'Pineuilh' to ensure you're sufficiently familiar with French language and geography to meet my arbitrary conditions of Frenchness. I'm not going to ask where you're really from if your physical presentation, your accent or something else collide with my presumptions about Frenchness and leave me with a sense of incongruity that I'd prefer you wrapped up for me in order to restore my equanimity. You should not be expected to move through the world differently so that it feels most comfortable – most familiar – to me. You can describe yourself however you want. I'm not the authority on what you are. I'm not the one who sets the criteria. I don't get to play the prospector, biting into you to check if your personal sense of your own identity is authentic. What do I care? What do I know?

Identity labels can connect or disconnect us, ground us or set us adrift, bring us closer to ourselves and one another or have us jealously policing other people in defence of a fragile, solipsistic world of our own construction. In London I once witnessed two football fans in a pub get into a fight over opposing team loyalties. Football fans can be weird that way (from my perspective at least), sometimes feeling such attachment to a particular club that they use what seems from over here like cultish language to talk about their team as a collective unit in which they are included. An in-group. A 'we'.

Peering over at two men I guessed were probably in their fifties as they elected to solve a problem by punching one another on a weekend afternoon, I marvelled. At how it so often seems that men carry a fundamental belief in their innate ability to fight, as though fighting competently isn't a learned skill like any other. As they threw punches with embarrassingly terrible form but a good deal of energetic investment, I also marvelled at the fact that each man attempted to physically impose the dominance of what they saw as their identity over the other. As though they had the truth pinched within their closed fists. As I watched their companions lunging in to separate them (one shouting with a combination of weariness and exasperation 'For fuck's sake, Neil, not again!') I thought *I'm not sure they'd want either of you lads on the team.*

Yet, what is it to me? Who am I to determine that 'we' is a word more fittingly belonging to the people who actually *play* for Arsenal or Manchester United or whoever else rather than the people who sit in pubs drinking lager and watching the matches for thirty years straight? What has their identity to do with me, or with my own, I consider as someone breaks a glass and Neil is dragged from the pub, purple in the face as his otherwise sedentary legs kick impotently and he shrieks something incomprehensible about 'the league'? Nothing at all. Their identity is not defined by my values, my experience, or my perception. These two drunken eejits were clearly wrong for exchanging blows over concepts of identity (as if winning the fight would somehow be relevant to actually settling the question) but not for cherishing that sense of their own identity in the first place. People can think of themselves however they please, and they do. The only problem is their behaviour towards 'the other'. It's presuming that the objectivity, the validity, the only acceptable narrative lies with 'my' team. It's presuming that you can observe collective identity markers or signals – a team jersey, an accent, a hoodie – and know the individual underneath. That you can look at them and know, through your sense of yourself, who they are.

There's the difficulty of inhabiting collective groups in a culture obsessed with individualism. We *must* do this in some sense. We can't take every interaction with every person as an entirely blank slate. We observe patterns, motifs, themes. We interpret people and situations by reference to what we know and what we have seen before. It's how we get things done.

When I'm at a gathering where there are small children present, they often wander over to me for some reason. I will suddenly feel conspicuously observed and look down only to lock eyes with the stare and open maw, slack in cogitation, of a toddler I've never met in my life. This toddler is frequently holding a half-eaten chip or other portable treasure in one protective little fist, considering me. Friends have laughed about this strange trend, knowing that for the most part I'm not the type to seek out the company of children or to feel particularly at ease around them. I'm never the woman in the room who makes a dash for every sweet, round-faced baby. The woman who is comfortably herself around little children. So why does it keep happening?

I'm five feet tall, significantly shorter than most adults I encounter, whatever their gender. I'm soft and therefore probably unintimidating-looking. My eyes are slightly larger and rounder than many people's. I know this because my optometrist tutted during my last eye test, saying, 'Yeah look your contact lenses aren't going to feel that comfortable because you just have a lot of eyeball. The surface area is large and lenses are less ... ahh ... wide. The curve is less wide [breathes deeply] . . . I mean.' He seemed to lose steam a bit after the phrase 'you just have a lot of eyeball'. I squinted toward the wall to check that his qualification was genuine but couldn't see properly without my uncomfortable, undersized lenses in.

What I'm saying is this – depending on who is looking, I might evoke a mother or I might evoke a child. I might look like the type of grown-up lady your mother instructs you to walk up to for help if you're six and you can't find her in the supermarket. I might look like I could have a brace of little children of my own, or like a Montessori teacher on her day off. I might look like a lot of things. Not considering myself from the outside, I don't know for certain what others see, and how those perceptions differ based on their own experience.

We all code for certain interpretations by manipulating our appearance to declare what we want it to as best we can. We signal for culture, gender, socio-economics, age demographic, religion or secularism. We try to build what we'd like people to see when they look at us. We behave publicly in ways designed to create the impression we want to create or mitigate the impression we don't. I do know, though, that someone else's conception of me does not take precedence over mine. There is no untouchable objectivity in their gaze. Performance is one element of identity, and it is among the first elements other people see, provided they're wearing their contact lenses. It does not follow that that is all there is.

Sensitivity around another person's identity is not disingenuous, enabling, coddling or political correctness. It is epistemic humility. It is acknowledgement of the vast realm of experience and understanding that lies beyond our own particular context. It is awareness that there is more to all of us than our immutable physical features, our accent or the band name on our T-shirt. It is a consciousness that there are ways in which we are fundamentally connected and there are elements of one another's experience that we can never truly understand. That there are ways to live in the world that extend beyond presuming everything is a nail just because we happen to be holding a hammer. That we should pursue as an ideal the practice of considering someone else in and of themselves rather than merely in narrow reference to 'me'.

We can hope that others grant us this in return and give us the space to be not merely what we say we are but something infinitely more complex. Something that changes. Something that encompasses what we come from but which is not reducible to the verdict of community, the product of ancestry or the vicissitudes of the zeitgeist. We could try to grant one another an empathy that extends far beyond labels but still has the breathing room to encompass them, which acknowledges why, in some contexts, they might matter a great deal. We are all more than the labels we live by, but there is no use denying that, for now, we still live in a world where happiness is white ink on white paper.

6

Poor

The best lack all conviction, while the worst
Are full of passionate intensity.
             – W. B. Yeats, 'The Second Coming'

'IT'S NOT YOUR PLACE to say things like that.' We are on the stairs again. They're carpeted with a bristling green floral print. If you focus too hard on it, you feel as though you're standing on the deck of a ship on a rough day, so I'm staring interestedly at my own shoes instead, my jaw set at a right angle. Getting a dressing down. Again. Why is it that so many of life's moments of friction seem to take place on stairs, in that liminal halfway place, floating somewhere between up and down in a location that is expressly designed to discourage lingering? Stairs are a route from one level to another. Stopping on them is a sign of indecision, crisis or interrupted momentum.

I spend far too much of my young life standing here in this tiered interregnum, an adult blocking my route, their spine prawned over while they attempt to talk sense into me before my foot can find the last step and gain the propulsion I crave. I'm a throwing arm drawn back, muscles singing in anticipation, and they're trying to tell me how the world works and that I need to get in line. Stand still. Be quiet.

This time I'm about ten and being told, essentially and always politely by my mother, to close the open gate that is my mouth and gain mastery over what keeps bolting out. Stop making things awkward for everyone. Don't ask the uncomfortable question. Don't say the thing we are all working so hard not to say for the sake of cohesion. The location of this particular intervention – one of many over the years – is my grandmother's stairs.

Though I'm ten, I can never quite shake the feeling that my grandmother is the worst person I know. I often occupy time spent in her house wondering why no one seems to talk about it much. When I notice a thing, I talk about it and have started to presume the opposite must hold true for others. They either don't notice or don't speak, or both. As far as I can tell, people talk about my behaviour all the time. Like it's a problem that should probably be solved for the benefit of all of us. This feels somewhat unjust, as though their focus might be more productively redirected elsewhere. But then it does appear as though there are elements to this that I can't entirely grasp. Things that linger, undeclared and heavy. Things that feel old, as though they were here before me. The air in my grandmother's house always feels taut as fabric, as though it isn't meant to fill your lungs all the way. It smells of Brasso and tension. You push against it to move around or you make yourself small to squeeze through the spaces it leaves but somehow you know, just know, to be cautious.

I had asked benignly – of the overheated room rather than any person in particular – why my grandmother never appeared to say anything nice to anybody, but especially to my mother, who as far as I can see takes such attentive care of her and who is, as I've been led to understand, her own daughter. This knowledge – that the people related to me may also be related to one another in various ways – is something I gained only in recent years and it's strange to think about.

My mother attends to her own mother with a care that has at its heart a sort of disturbing vigilance. It seethes and thrums with anticipation and something like terror. Like something hog-tied just inside an open door or a shuddering creature trapped in the eyeline of a predator. It is the awareness of a daughter who has never been allowed to believe that she has done anything right. Who has never been granted a moment of peace or validation. It is the atmosphere that radiates from a daughter who cannot decide if she needs her mother or hates her. Maybe both. There is no love at all in this house. It is salted earth. I don't yet understand this but I can feel it all the same. The feeling imposes itself like the pinch of an unwanted grip.

As a result, when she is in this house, my mother – normally so gentle and prim – sits on the edge of my grandmother's least favourite living-room armchair with the posture of someone ready to jump up at a nano-second's notice. This is the posture of someone who questions everything about herself, all the way down to whether she deserves to sit in a chair. My grandmother, meanwhile, is planted deep in the abdomen of her own favoured chair like someone who may need to be removed from it with a crowbar.

From this chair, she tells us all what the world is and how it works. She tells us who we are and what we are permitted to think. She left school at fourteen to care for her younger siblings and is angered by anything she does not understand. She has the rage of someone carried off young by fate and never retrieved. She is afraid, but I don't know that yet. All I can see is a biting intolerance for everyone around her and a bottomless need that clutches at you indiscriminately the closer you stand to it.

My question is voiced during a brief pause in the list my grandmother was dictating. It is the week's errands my mother would need to do for her. She never says please or thank you, and my mother is frightened of her. Even I can see that. There is some-thing coiled within my grandmother that seeps into all of us, out and out through everyone close to her. Lake-dark and teeming. I don't like to be alone in her company.

It was most likely innocent. My question, that is. A query sprouted from observation over time, that my grandmother does not say nice things to people. To my mother, whom I have observed to be very nice, and deserving of words that are nice. This made it precisely explosive enough to render everyone distinctly uncomfortable. I feel the room narrow in a clench but can't interpret any information that may emerge from the contraction apart from *Ah . . . I'm in trouble again, so.* What was previously a small, trinket-heavy living room rendered low by the muck-brown hues of 90s interiors dictum is suddenly a sphincter straining to pass something painfully dry and oversized. When a ten-year-old child loudly asks, 'Why don't you ever say nice things to anybody?' in a credulous, interrogative tone, her small, moonish face unbesmirched by any trace of provocation or deliberate shit-stirring, adults are prompted to feel things they'd really rather not.

In moments like these I was often led gently, silently by the elbow through the debris of my inappropriate questions and out to the privacy and purgatory of the stairs so that my mother could look me in the eye and make an appeal to what she considered my better nature. Would I not just stop? I was making people uncomfortable. I was reflecting poorly on her. It wasn't my place. I wondered why articulating the truth – or even gesturing too close to it – was considered so much more objectionable than the mere fact of the truth itself, but hadn't the words or concepts to form this idea.

I felt the dissonance like a flat palm on my back without being able to whirl round to clasp or name it, and longed for the day when I was big enough to lean back on my own weight and resist being led from rooms, elbow aloft, against my will. Like a dog whose house training its owner is still unconfident about or a queasy father-to-be being escorted, grey in the face and whimpering, from the birthing suite by a criminally overworked nurse just as all the real stuff is starting to happen.

One day about four years later, while being called to task on my grandmother's stairs once again, though more firmly and with less patience now I was definitely old enough to know precisely the discomfort I was exposing, I had a profound moment of realisation. The kind of sudden awareness that lands upon you like the sharp slap of a snowball unmaking itself against your head. There, in the ambiguous in-between on the same agitated green carpet, the dissonance finally revealed itself. The one that had always rendered me churlish after my stair-lectures, feeling as though I'd arrived at a knife fight holding a rubber chicken and come out the worse. The invisible hand on my back, pushing me reluctantly away into nowhere and nothing.

When someone (even my mother, whom I loved, and who loved me) told me it wasn't my place to say something, what they were really saying was that I was making things difficult for *them*. Dragging something rotten into full view when others would prefer or needed to ignore it. That it is the person who points

out wrongdoing, and not the act of committing wrongdoing itself, which makes it untenable for people – in
this case a family – to coexist comfortably together.

In the context of Irish culture and working-class
Irish culture especially, the truth or falsity of what you
were saying was not what people cared about. What
mattered was whether people think that *you* have the
right to make the observation. The source mattered at
least as much as the statement or question, usually
more. The rules changed depending on who was
speaking. This is perhaps unsurprising for the Ireland
of my childhood – a country on the cusp of realising
the catastrophic consequences of raising generations
of children whose silence was so deeply enforced as a
virtue. For all that the public conversation later ques-
tioned why more didn't speak up when the
unconscionable extent of institutional abuse became
clear. Nobody wanted to hear it. A child must be
granted a voice before they can use it. They must be
allowed to feel that their voice is for using, and will
be heard. As a child grows up there is no point at
which rigorously enforced submissiveness disappears
and is suddenly replaced by a healthy relationship with
assertiveness and self-respect. Irish children were raised
within a culture of blind deference to authority and
taught that individual worth lay in silence and
conformity. Irish adults reflect these values. As a result,
many of us struggle to assert ourselves and compound
the problem.

I was an angry child, veering pendulously between this silent submission and alienating people by saying what no one else seemed willing to. It seems likely now that I was groping about for truth – or at least honesty – because I could see it set before us all like a plate of rotting food, ignored by adults who were equipped to do something about it.

I couldn't grasp the double life of silence and pretence in which those around me engaged, and I was interested. Interested in why someone would choose to profess a belief ('smoking is bad and people shouldn't do it'/ 'telling lies is wrong'/ 'I care about my family') but act in direct opposition to that belief, then demand that I respect them for being older and wiser despite all evidence that wisdom was generally in chronically short supply. As though I should accept the idea that our words contain more truth than our behaviour.

I was interested in the fear that seemed to have my family mincing around one another on their eyelashes to avoid making a sound. The tension that kept everyone around me more invested in safeguarding an illusion than describing things as they really were and blowing it all apart. It is better – surely – to live in a wreckage together than to feel locked inside it with someone who insists you describe the mess in palatial language because the reality is impossible for them to live with. At least a wreckage might be salvaged.

I didn't know it at the time but this was my earliest experience of what Plato and Aristotle called *akrasia*.

It is a beautifully concise term, denoting that 'weakness of will' (or 'incontinence', if you want to be a little less generous and more liquid about it) whereby we consciously ignore insights we know perfectly well that we should acknowledge and retain. We act against our better judgement to our own detriment and in ways which buy us short-term comfort yet ultimately erode our self-respect. It is when we know how we should act, but don't. The knowing and the refusing to know. The choices we make that result in us disliking and losing faith in ourselves. The moment when you realise you've eaten enough to fill you but keep going regardless, as though you might power through the gnawing awareness that this eating you do is not really about hunger at all. The moment the thought crystallises across your awareness: *you've done this a lot lately and it is making you feel bad.* It's the quiver of insight when that recurring voice tells you your asymmetric friendship may not be entirely the fault of the bad friend. You are to blame for failing to tell them honestly how you feel and you've made a coward of yourself.

In psychology, akrasia is studied in relation to things like motivation and the ability to regulate our behaviours and emotions. It considers the emotional and cognitive processes that are intrinsic to changing our behaviour. In philosophical terms, it is a state of dissonance which gives rise to all of that. The discrepancy between what we claim to want and what we do.

It is the state by which you become a person who claims to hold a belief but does not live by it, generating a gorge between what you claim to think and how you actually live which is wide enough to fall into. Complaining about a situation you know you could change (even in small ways) if you really desired to trudge through the discomfort required to get somewhere better. Choosing to behave as though you are powerless in situations where you could exercise some agency and consequently disempowering yourself. It's the flickering realisation that if everyone you date is a commitment-phobic kleptomaniac who steals your hand towels, the common denominator there is you (and arguably the high quality of your towels). It is continuing to make the same bad choices long after noticing the pattern. Akrasia – we act in contravention to reason.

There is so much incentive to allow these sorts of realisations to slip from our grasp – to convince ourselves that ignoring them is not in itself a choice. To choose what feels like an easier life right now, the cost of which seems to be elevated discomfort, distress and lack of self-respect in perpetuity. The knowledge that we are living a dishonest life and can see ourselves doing it. Prioritising how we appear to others over self-respect. In this way, we often choose to perform an identity that we know perfectly well is corrosive to ourselves for the benefit of other people. If we do this for long enough, we no longer recognise a self outside that identity. We become brittle, one-dimensional, defensive. We lose ourselves.

The feeling this generates is one I came to understand later, in adulthood. Distaste, alienation and ultimately cowardice, it persists until we address the thing we are ignoring. The awareness that looms itchily over our ability to immerse in the moment, robbing us of ease. Even when we have the realisation and even if we manage to look straight into it like someone burning their retinas gawking at an eclipse because Amazon didn't deliver the glasses on time, our grip on our own epiphany is limited.

What impacts with the force of a projectile into the windpipe at breakfast time often evaporates from our awareness by dinner. We can have a profound moment of existential realisation, shift about in our chair a bit, and then go back to scrolling videos of cats looking stern in funny costumes, safe in the knowledge that our internal furniture will have re-established its usual orientation if we just sit here long enough with our legs going numb. 'This Maine Coon is dressed like a taco and he is *not* happy about it!'

We're capable of great insight and profundity but we're also weak, tired, chronically overstimulated and overcaffeinated, easily distracted and permanently – if barely consciously – stressed about a world that is increasingly difficult to recognise and untenably expensive to live in. Besides, we'll do almost anything to avoid discomfort, and goodness knows there's nothing more agonising than taking a good long look at yourself.

Even as a child, I wanted what I have always professed to value most in life – that thing prompting all those liminal childhood interludes on various staircases. All those interventions designed to snap me into smaller pieces that might fit better into the existing environment rather than consider how suffocating that environment was for all of us. I wanted autonomy. The freedom to choose for myself. To do, think and say what I choose (even in instances where nobody else finds what I think or say relevant or important, because I'm not thinking or saying it to please them). Even when someone else determines that it isn't my place. Especially in those instances, since an assigned place implies an inability to move without permission and I learned early that you cannot always rely on those in authority to earn or respect the power they wield.

What I carried out of childhood was the knowledge that in some situations, our autonomy can be articulated only in direct contradiction to our fear. That is where we find it – in the din and juddering impact of an 'ought' hammering against an 'is'. In recognising akrasia as a supremely human condition and tendency and refusing to run screaming from it back into a place of comfort and palliation. In the choices our feelings resist – not in the choices that feel pleasant, or comfortable, but in the horrible, embarrassing discomfort we endure for sound reasons. In true vulnerability. Often, we know precisely what it is that we need to do. We know what is meaningful to us as opposed to what is merely familiar, safe, easy or expected. We know what we need but we are afraid of the costs of being seen to try or to fail.

The adults I grew up around were not equipped to ask these sorts of questions. They were trapped within a cycle of constant stress which locked them into the immediate present and made the future something they felt incapable of anticipating or preparing for. All of them, in various respects, were unable to escape the cycle of mental health problems, abuse and addiction that dictated the conditions under which they lived. My mother was an exceptional person, escaping a cycle of abuse, or distancing herself from it, and somehow electing not to perpetuate it. I've never been able to fully understand how she came to be something other than merely the product of her environment. How she knew, without any robust example, that there were other ways to live and other ways to conceive of herself. She nurtured my brother and me and was somehow capable of deep kindness despite having experienced so little of it from anyone else. She instilled in us both an ambition that, statistically speaking, the children of a single mother had no business aspiring to. Her ambition for us was sometimes fierce – fierce enough to drown out rumination on the predicted outcomes for kids in our situation – but my mother remained locked within an abusive relationship with her own mother until she died. She adopted the role of carer despite progressive demand and intensity for the entire duration of her adult life.

When I was seventeen and in my final year of school, my grandmother was sectioned and hospitalised in a psychiatric facility. Emma visited her every day, bringing fresh clothing along with anything else she might need. Carrying in foods that might tempt my grandmother to eat even as she evaporated, body and mind, listening to her extensive speeches about how her doctors were certainly trying to poison her, and how bad things from the past came to get her in the night. Through all of this, my mother advocated for her, worried about her, cared for her as tenderly as someone else might tend a loving mother at her most frightened, ill and vulnerable. More than once, Emma challenged the decisions of psychiatrists, who had the ultimate decision on my grandmother's care while she was hospitalised. Their education deeply intimidated my mother. I saw how much it took for her to question their authority and ask to be considered and consulted in relation to my grandmother's treatment. She resisted their decision to give her mother repeated courses of ECT (electroconvulsive therapy) when my grandmother seemed only to become more and more mentally absent, ill and frail.

My mother was often at the hospital, and when I did see her, she spoke about my grandmother constantly. This is understandable, but I was seventeen and should not have been her primary sounding board and emotional outlet. This behaviour is called parentification, when a parent without the emotional support of a partner places a child in the role of the absent spouse, relying on them as they might an adult, discussing difficulties or stresses with them which they are too young to navigate, requiring a child to act as confidant or mediator and as a result, to grow up prematurely and leave them with a sense that they are responsible for the parent.

Parentification can also take the form of a child filling the physical caregiving role of a parent – cooking, cleaning, going out to work or, as in the case of my grandmother, being placed in a role as carer to younger siblings. The consensus in psychology literature seems to suggest that while parentification can sometimes result in resilient adults who can problem-solve and adapt in difficult circumstances, it can also result in children growing up to experience chronic stress, increased propensity toward mental health issues, and difficulties in adult relationships. All of this is likely true and yet it is not particularly helpful in the context of poverty. In an ideal world, a child should never be placed in the role of an adult. In a non-ideal world, it may be a means by which families continue to function.

I wanted to help Emma. It became my role and I do not regret it. She twice brought me with her to the hospital to visit my grandmother. Not all areas of the psychiatric ward were gender-segregated. On my way to the bathroom on the second visit, a young male patient appeared suddenly beside me, shoved me aggressively against a wall and groped me. I had seen him on a previous visit, dark, unwashed hair lying flat on his head and with a look in his eyes that frightened me. It suggested that he wasn't in the room at all, but entirely somewhere else. Somewhere unspeakably terrible. He walked repeatedly in circles, muttering to himself. I was so shocked to find myself suddenly against a wall with a stranger's hands on me that I couldn't speak at all while it was happening.

It felt like I was immobilised there for a long time but it must only have been moments. He jumped away when someone rounded the corner. When I got back to my grandmother's room, I glanced at my mother's stressed expression, and sat down silently. 'You stay here and they'll kill you,' my grandmother said, knowingly. It occurred to me, not for the first time, that life was spectacularly volatile and frightening.

I never spoke to my mother about what had happened. At the time, there wasn't room for it. 'You fucking stupid little bitch,' the man had hissed into my ear with a sour blast of long-unbrushed teeth. His words landed on me with the violence of his hands; it felt briefly, bizarrely unjust that he would say this to me, as though I had harmed him, and he hated me. A man had never touched me in a sexual way before. I was enraged by the fact that this was my first experience. I was repulsed by the fear that meant I cowered there silently, shutting down and allowing him to violate me out of utter panic. I could not find autonomy when

I needed it and it made me feel weak. Pathetic. The experience served only to confirm my presumption that the world was a dysfunctional and unpredictable place, a place to fear, and that I was ultimately on my own in it. On the way home from the hospital, my mother looked straight ahead through the windscreen. Something complicated passed over her face too quickly for me to read it and she said, 'I don't want you to come on any more visits with me.' 'But why?' I asked, relief loosening an iron band in my throat that I hadn't realised was there. 'It's not your job, and it shouldn't be,' she said. I didn't say anything.

This combination of rage and silence was what I carried with me into Trinity College Dublin, Ireland's elite university. Arguably, it fuelled my propulsion there in the first place. That rage to escape, to be elevated, and to fulfil my mother's wishes for me. Trinity is an institution in which I spent over a decade of my life studying, on and off. A sanctum sanctorum of Irish academia and middle-class sensibility, it has long funnelled the literary and intellectual elite of Irish society through the solid wooden door of its famed eighteenth-century Front Arch. Oscar Wilde. Edmund Burke. George Berkeley. A few Nobel Laureates and numerous canonical Irish writers. Mary Robinson, former Irish president (the first woman in the job) and former UN High Commissioner for Human Rights. Samuel Beckett is often apparently misquoted as having described the university's students as the cream of

Ireland – 'rich and thick'. At least you'll quickly be told that it's a misquote if you repeat it within the 431-year-old walls of Trinity. The description stuck, nonetheless. It is the sort of place heavily featured in novels by writers like Sally Rooney (who went to Trinity) so that you have decent context for the more intellectual, infuriating or status-conscious characters. It is the alma mater of people with names like Tarquin who sit under trees straining to grow a moustache and pretending to read Proust in the hope that someone – anyone – will consider them sufficiently erudite to warrant rushing over to ask their opinion on Israel and Palestine. It is my alma mater, where I too hoped to seem mysterious and erudite and have my opinion solicited, only without the moustache.

There's plenty of room in the world for the Tarquins along with everyone else but if you've just got off the bus from Limerick with your packed lunch sweating in a plastic box in your backpack, you might feel a touch out of your depth. You might feel as though you took a Panadol for a headache only to look carefully at the bottle and realise that you've accidentally swallowed your dog's colon medicine. It is not entirely the fault of elite universities – those across the Western world are caught in what Ned Flanders from *The Simpsons* might describe as 'a real dilly of a pickle'. They need to exude inclusivity and make every effort to do this without undermining their modus operandi – to produce the very best and brightest, the young people who will go on to shape policy and culture. To create the tastemakers and the gatekeepers. The decision-makers. The very appeal of such institutions depends upon reputations built on elitism.

Academic high achievement and familiarity with the social mores of people who endorse and inhabit what is considered the modern iteration of 'high culture', which is value-laden and decidedly not working class, are the bare necessities for success within, if not entry to, such places. Chess rather than first-person shooter video games. Concept fusion restaurants blending French and Ethiopian cuisines, and not KFC. Vegan trainers whose industrial-scale farming impact we don't think about too deeply and fair-trade coffee in a keep cup brought from home. These institutions nurture the kind of people who will watch you drink a McDonald's coffee as though you were eating a whole rotisserie chicken with your bare hands during a funeral service. The accessories and hobbies of those whose in-group status is dependent on signalling the 'right' and most enlightened values do not include cheap corporate coffee and supermarket rotisserie chickens. Unless they're from M&S or, in the UK, Waitrose. Then maybe.

No amount of pronouns in email signatures, rainbow flags or public seminars on women in the workplace can make elite universities egalitarian. This is a significant problem for them, as the institutions generating the very values that undermine their business model. What they have to offer depends entirely on their *not* being accessible to everyone. It depends upon serious barriers to entry and the existence and reinforcement of hierarchy. Everything else is window dressing – elite universities are tasked with sprucing things at the margins to make largely cosmetic efforts toward accessibility. Just enough to prevent undermining the product they are ultimately there to sell and which, in their defence, is also why they operate initiatives designed to improve access to young people from deprived backgrounds. We tacitly believe that elite university education is a proxy for social advancement. That this sort of education, and the circles to which it grants students access, is a reliable way to counteract or reverse the adverse conditions in which poor kids grow up. In reality, education is only part of the equation, and often the easiest to point to.

While young people from a variety of backgrounds can theoretically gain entry to the sorts of educational institutions which give them access to significant social mobility, they usually don't and when they do, they often struggle. This is particularly blatant at Russell Group universities – institutions including Cambridge, Oxford, King's College London and Durham – in the UK, where social mobility is far more constipated within society as a whole than it is in Ireland.

According to the *Guardian*, working-class students comprise around 20 per cent of undergraduate students across the twenty-four Russell Group universities. For postgraduate students, the number is lower.

Among professionals in occupations like law, journalism, sport and medicine (also MPs and High Court judges) a disproportionate number were educated at private schools and/or at Oxford or Cambridge despite the fact that only around 1 per cent of the British population attends one of those two universities, while just 7 per cent of the population were educated in fee-paying schools.

Single-parent households experience the highest deprivation rates in Ireland and so children born to them are far more likely to be classified as disadvantaged. Children raised in single-parent families in Ireland are twice as likely to experience poverty as those born into two-parent families and four times as likely to experience consistent poverty, a combination of both income poverty and material deprivation. This generates a level of psychological strain and focus on urgent needs in both children and their caregiver, which obviously makes education a less imminent priority in both the short and longer term. It is hardly a surprise then that children from single-parent families consistently achieve lower educational attainment and occupational status in adulthood. Poverty begets poverty. If you're cold, hungry, living under threat of violence or raised in otherwise unstable and erratic conditions, education is a peripheral consideration at best and attending third-level education is often not an accessible or relevant option.

In Ireland, according to Ireland's Higher Education Authority, in 2020/21 one in ten higher education students came from a background that qualifies as disadvantaged while one in five came from affluent backgrounds. Unsurprisingly, a much higher proportion of affluent students progress to postgraduate study than their disadvantaged counterparts. A very small minority of undergraduates enrolling at Trinity College Dublin and University College Dublin – the two major Dublin universities – come from disadvantaged backgrounds.

Crucially, I'm not making a gendered point here but one about class, which supersedes gender in this respect. Tarquin can just as easily be an Emily or a Saoirse or a Charlotte. Women account for 54.5 per cent of the overall student population in Ireland. We are a majority – not in every discipline or department, but overall among people educated at third level in the context of both Ireland and the UK. A working-class male student will generally have a much harder time making his way through an elite institution than a middle-class female student. The environment and mores will be familiar to her in a way they cannot be to someone who was raised within an entirely different social and socio-economic context, one whose signals (most of which are unconsciously sent) act as a significant disadvantage in elite environments. She will have gained the intangible skills to maximise her advantage from parents who come from a similar background. Elite universities desperately want to be seen to include and elevate women – the backgrounds those women come from are largely a secondary consideration. Optically, women are women for the most part.

Emily, Saoirse and Charlotte are pretty good at advocating for themselves and are present within elite universities in high enough numbers to do that effectively. Working-class young people – especially those from backgrounds that qualify as disadvantaged – are not, making advocating for their needs and advantage significantly more difficult. Those from lower-income immigrant backgrounds face the same difficulty, usually with added challenges, though like students from disadvantaged and working-class backgrounds, they lack the language and the necessary environmental habituation to work the system effectively. As a result their struggle is frequently conducted in isolation, leaving them feeling adrift in what is ultimately an alien environment.

When young people from working-class backgrounds do find themselves within the dissonant atmosphere fostered by such places, they often languish, feeling academically or socially overwhelmed, or both. They lack the means or context to gain ground quickly enough to keep pace with peers like Tarquin and Charlotte and this tends not to be officially acknowledged because it would entail tackling the idea that, in some instances, higher-level education is not always conducive to the flourishing of young people from disadvantaged backgrounds. That education alone may not be sufficient route to social mobility. To acknowledge their struggle would be to actively acknowledge their difference. In ideological environments where socio-economic differences are so often overlooked and equality is constantly confused with parity, flipping that rock may expose something ugly beneath.

Tarquin has his own struggles as a young person navigating his way through the world and a person who is likely to be carrying the weight of significant social and parental expectation. These challenges are legitimate but they will not include lack of social or academic preparation for the environment of an elite university. He looks and sounds like he belongs precisely because he does belong. There is no categorical or exceptional dissonance which impedes his route through. Tarquin passes. His voice is the institutional voice. His manners are the manners of the institution. The culture he grew up within is the culture in which he remains.

When I was growing up, I hated the lexicon and accent of where I came from because I understood that committing to it would declare to others not just what I was but all the many things I *wasn't*. My mother painstakingly and deliberately trained every long, breathy, interrogative regional vowel out of my speech. Sometimes an accent which is less responsive to change based on environment is a feature associated with autism. Yet I don't really think that is why I sound, as one reader of the *Irish Times* once so eloquently emailed me, 'like all those other elite journo twats I hear on the radio'.

The Limerick accent would sometimes creep in and follow me home from school, curling my tongue and reverberating between my teeth. 'Wan' instead of 'one'. 'Swang' instead of 'swan'. 'That youngfla' instead of 'that boy'. My mother would catch every stray intonation and colloquialism, gently but firmly squashing it. She wanted me to be untraceable to any particular part of Ireland in the belief that this would make me more socially mobile and ease my route into and through middle-class environments. My mother was entirely right. It did. A plummy voice will hide the fact (for a while, at least) that you unironically like KFC and think McDonald's coffee is no less flavoursome (or otherwise) than Pret's. It will help you pass long enough to climb the ladder.

Now, I can appreciate Hiberno-English, which Irish lexicographer T. P. Dolan describes in his *The Dictionary of Hiberno-English* as having 'its own grammar, so obviously different in several ways from Standard English Grammar that it may appear to be a "wrong grammar", such as that Seamus Heaney "decently relapses into".' The 'it would be' rather than the less lyrical and flatter 'it is'. This appreciation may have come from eventually gaining access to those places I venerated in my youth – middle- and upper middle-class environments like universities and broadsheet newspapers. Being surrounded by the received pronunciation (both British and Irish) that in my callowness I mistook for good breeding and intellectual depth.

Before I had the chance to look behind that door and find the people drinking out of keep cups with an air of quiet sanctimony to be ultimately the same as everyone else, just with different clothes and accents. I loathed the reedy, mysterious and lyrical character of a Limerick accent – emphysemic – which has generated its own particular colloquial phrasing, just like any other. Limerick people always sound as though they have a secret they enjoy holding over you.

One of the most frustrating aspects of adult life is the realisation that we sometimes (or often) need to relearn lessons we have already taken pains to teach ourselves. I walked through Front Arch that first time early one October morning, my boots knocking sharp echoes against the thick, cold stone walls of the stately old entryway like rumours, haunted by the ghost of an angry child who grew up under profound uncertainty. Who learned to expect judgement from people whose role in her life would ideally have been one of guidance and support. Who encountered kindness with suspicion and always felt undeserving. Who had yet to learn how people who value learning for its own sake engage with one another and how to (verbally) cut the legs from under an egalitarian Tarquin or Emily when their right-side-of-history open-mindedness reflexively contracts like a sneer around unenlightened working-class tastes.

Getting into Trinity was the greatest achievement of my life to that point. It had all the triumph of slipping a cold knife between the warm ribs of fate. Despite believing I understood what the conditions of my birth meant in terms of my future, I walked through the door as a statistical anomaly and naively presumed that pattern would just continue. That there was something special in me that would ensure it did, despite my deep feelings of perpetual inadequacy. It may have been a harder walk had I understood then that I was a member of a category of people who had very little chance of excelling in this sort of environment. When my present and past became too alienated from one another and the words began to move on the page in my second year, I decided to take a year out of Trinity and go home to Limerick. To work in a bookshop in the hope of retrieving what I considered my lost sanity if possible, and my value. Without academic achievement – or the momentum of striving toward it – I felt value-less. My first two years since entering Trinity had featured significantly more striving than achieving.

Nobody knew that I couldn't read after that first time in the library when the words exited the page, scratching an erratic route out of my reach like a trail of aggravated ants. Something about the words deserting me felt so close to madness that there was a shame deep inside the fact of it that I could not navigate. I felt the dry heat of 'who does she think she is, studying philosophy?' radiating from people I knew at home. 'You'll be a teacher so – lovely!' they'd beam, appearing not to know what philosophy was.

People often confused it for the study of human minds. 'That would be ironic,' I'd think, having recently lost my own, but there was something more ironic still. Sashaying off to that fancy university to study a fruity discipline (which would presumably render me unemployable and a further burden to my mother) only to shuffle home two summers later, unqualified and illiterate.

I told a classmate that I was taking a year out of my degree programme and going home. She was the sort of person who always spoke at the decibel level of a small aircraft and on more than one occasion wore a bucket hat indoors, presumably in an attempt to be ironic. A lot, in short. While hoovering up a vanilla malt as we sat together in a red pleather booth in the grim Stillorgan branch of Eddie Rockets one afternoon, she advised strongly against my taking time off. No advice had been solicited but then that rarely acts as the impediment it probably should. 'Honestly?' She looked off into the distance, ponderously. 'I think you lack the ambition to come back and finish what you started. I think you should work on having the drive to push through hard things. I'm seriously worried you won't make anything of your life if you leave.' I looked down into my onion rings, which were now flaccid with sitting out so long, and considered.

The middle-class response to a statement like this is to feel that an act of aggression has been perpetrated against you and possibly to seek mediation through some higher authority like a teacher or casually passing legal representative. Or to feign a phone call and leave, then never acknowledge the existence of the offending individual ever again. It is the registering of deep affront mitigated by avoidance of direct confrontation. The working-class response is either to punch the person (though that's a reaction more often favoured by men), tell them to fuck themselves utterly off, or to bank it. Being too repressed and illiterate for all-out violence at the time, the comment settled under my skin, oily and cold, confirming my perception of myself as weak and valueless. Mostly, I just felt tired. Being well accustomed to having my potential described for me by other people as though they had expertise on the subject, I went back to my room and eventually chose the third option. The only one available to me which might motivate rather than exsanguinate me. The option to file this moment in your mind in the section titled 'Historic Resentments: Underestimation'. To feed it into a furnace that has burnt livid inside your scorched gut as far back as you can remember and leave it in there to generate the energy you'll certainly need for other things.

The day I graduated from Trinity College with a doctorate several years later, I thought primarily of my mother who had worked two jobs to push me through Front Arch and helped keep me inside it. Who had borrowed money from the credit union to get me out of a bad school and into one that might propel me out of Limerick and into Trinity, and who was still paying that money back every month until she got sick. The woman who filled my summers with W. B. Yeats and Tolstoy, Shakespeare and Jane Austen, and who let me watch *Buffy the Vampire Slayer* as long as I'd done all my homework, even though she said it seemed a bit violent and silly. Who took me hard by the shoulders when I relayed to her what my classmate had told me about myself and said, '*Do not* let anyone else tell you where you belong. *Never* hand them that power,' because she had long since stopped telling me herself.

It had been years since the last time we stood together in mutual opposition on my grandmother's stairs, when I was pushing to the end of adolescence and my mother told me quietly, once again, that it was not my place to say what I thought. To say 'This is not how it should be' in the vicinity of adults with the power to do something about it. Something tore within me and I responded in a vicious whisper, so my grandmother would not hear through the door, petulant with poorly repressed frustration, 'Surely my place is wherever *I choose to put myself?!*' It was a question and it wasn't. Emma looked at me as though I had slapped her. As though the ceiling had come in on top of us. And after a long pause she replied, 'Well. And maybe it is.' My mother never again jostled me out through the living-room door and onto those stairs. Never again decided for me where my place was.

It was she who followed me through that graduation day, standing just out of view like a spectral memory. The woman whose disapproval had no pliancy when she felt I didn't try hard enough. The woman whose arms were wide open when I limped home after that second year of university unable to open a book, doubled over by my own sense of failure and displacement. 'The words will come back,' she said gently, folding me in with quiet certainty. This woman who could be both harder and softer than anyone. 'I know it. Wait and see.'

My mother didn't live to see the fructification of her ambitions for me. She would never know what security felt like, and her own mother, who never was outside the centre of things, outlived Emma only by a couple of weeks, dying in her eighties. I searched for feeling on hearing this news but could find none. All of my grief was for Emma. As I waited for the commencement ceremony to start, clad in the garish, too-big, too-long robe of a doctoral graduate and holding the goofy mortar-board cap pinched in my hand, I thought of my mother. I also thought briefly of that classmate all those years before, delineating the bounds of my potential with far more ease and immediacy than she could coax a thick vanilla malt up the length of an unwilling straw through capillary action.

I don't think there was any coincidence in the fact that her image imposed itself on the moment as I sat in the aged elegance of Trinity College's public theatre. Beneath the portrait of one of the university's most exalted graduates, the philosopher George Berkeley, listening through the solemn ritual of a Latin ceremony that surely only a handful of the several hundred people in the room could follow. Because you don't forget the people who affirm your bone-deep feeling that you don't deserve to get in (wherever 'in' happens to be), or once in, who remind you that you need to do more than others to stay. That you need to prove your right to be in a place that was never designed to admit you despite the gratitude you feel for being there. A place where you must learn to read all over again.

I've thought many times before and since that I had put that baffled, angry child to bed, and it is always humbling and frightening to find her again occasionally, lurking darkly and huffily in unexpected places where I feel I don't belong, called forth from standing on the stairs of an unstable past to limit herself for fear of being excluded or found wanting. I find her distasteful, unevolved and abhorrent. An emotional embodiment of my own failure to become, and to stay, better. More. My failure to accept the progress that I've made; to overcome the story that belonging is something other people grant you.

That child is a tether to a past self I don't want to recognise. Because the reality is that I don't now live a life resembling the life of my youth. That pugnacious girl responds to threats that are not quite there and anticipates catastrophes which are less imminent – or less assured – than they once were. I've achieved what my mother would have considered 'elevation'. I pass (mostly) for middle class. Or can when I choose to, at least in Ireland. Not for working class though, probably. My mother made sure of that. (I keep Pepsi Max in my keep cup.).

I still find myself bracing for some manner of catastrophe that doesn't come and seeking evidence that I don't belong. Some things are difficult to unlearn. There is a tautness in my gut that is waiting for my gentle, comfortable life to reveal itself as something else. Something harder. Because people like me usually don't get to live a life like this. A life that allows for mental space to stretch. A life not lived in an attitude of defence.

I think of the struggle my mother endured; her strain to achieve basic independence. Penury. Abuse. A total lack of support and two children utterly depending on her. Working two jobs until she got too sick to maintain it all, and then dying of cancer in her fifties. I think of this, and I look at my preposterous life of relative comfort and safety, my ability to write for a living. My space to ruminate, to choose for myself, to say 'no' when I want to. To describe what I see without seeking permission. I feel guilty. I feel grateful. I feel like someone who has bolted, spooked and breathless, through an open gate and carries a constant gnawing fear that eventually someone with authority will appear to drag me back through it. That the natural order will re-establish itself.

My upbringing taught me that people do not generally get what they deserve. People get what they get. The better-off don't enjoy what they have based on merit alone. People sleeping on the street aren't there based on some moral failure or on lack of merit. We work within the parameters into which we are born. Sometimes the odds are so heavily stacked against a person that overcoming them is virtually impossible, and it often takes more than one generation to change conditions.

Where there is rapid change – within a generation – there will be displacement. A breach between what you come from and where you end up. A sense of liminality and fear that never quite dissipates and comes from having understood that a couple of stumbles at an adverse moment can have you falling forever. So you keep an eye on the ground to keep from tripping.

I don't 'deserve' the life I have now. It has not occurred by cosmic realignment, through the magnetic sophistry of manifestation or through fate. I have it because of choices my mother made despite her circumstances, because of choices I made despite mine, and – crucially – because the wind blew the right way at the right time, and I got lucky. I was lucky to have someone to open their arms to catch me when I did stumble. Therein lies the fear – the wind can change. I've seen what can happen when it does.

I've realised since moving from London to Australia – where life is cheaper, slower and closer to the class structure of Ireland than the series of progressively smaller containment rooms that are the British class system – that this fear, this vulnerability, will probably never leave me. The fear of poverty, of obscurity, of shrinking out of being. Being taken out onto the stairs and told to reshape myself to fit the expectations and comfort of other people. There is no level of safety or stability I can reach that will rebuff the cold draught of childhood whispering at the back of my neck. No level of education that can undo it or eradicate the mark it leaves behind. It is a vulnerability, and it's a strength. The wind can change but we can too. I've seen it. Doors can be locked, but they can also be kicked in.

*

Class is creeping back into mainstream public conversation in a promising way. For a decade or so there, it seemed that race and gender were the only lenses through which it was acceptable to view social issues. The result has been some progress but also a lot of bolstering of the power of people who were already doing alright. A lot of empowering people who may not have needed it most. A lot of judging the validity of what someone says based on how entitled we decide they are to speak.

When the collective identity category we are associated with (by choice or imposition) is the most important element of who we are in public contexts, a hierarchy of voices naturally emerges. That is how it has always been – nothing about it feels particularly progressive. Socio-economics stretches across all other categories. Failure to recognise this is how we end up with women educated to master's level convinced that their promotion at work is the cold face of the fight for equality while a boy who fell through the holes in the foster care system can't access medical care because he doesn't have a fixed address.

Conversations on gender and race are critically important – the fact that we are collectively having those conversations does represent progress. However, there is an opportunity for solidarity and advocacy among people who may look different from one another, have different reproductive organs or come from different cultures, and we are still, for the most part, failing to recognise the commonalities and organise around them. Failing to see one another as more than the sum of our parts. It is worth considering who benefits from that. Whose interests it serves. It isn't the people who suffer most and possess the least.

7

Emerging

*. . . a certain degree of intelligence is required to be able to
know that a man knows not, and we must push against a
door to know whether it be bolted against us or no.*
— Michel de Montaigne, *Essays*

BACK WHEN I WAS a philosophy teaching assistant, I
delivered weekly seminars to small groups of undergraduate students. They would attend their lectures
with whichever academic was convening the specific
course they were taking. Then they would shuffle duti-
fully into a little classroom on the fifth floor of the
Arts Block to spend an hour or two with me. Our
seminars were generally scheduled on Tuesday after-
noons and Thursday mornings at the especially
barbarous time of 9 a.m. Arguably, it was not the ideal
time to discuss the philosophical ideas and concepts
they'd been introduced to that week or to engage in
critical analysis of the assigned reading material. But
it was when the room was free, so.

I don't mind admitting that I wasn't particularly good at the job. On the first week of classes I got the times mixed up and was about thirty minutes late, running panting into a room of seriously underwhelmed young faces. I was also only about five or so years older than the students, significantly younger than the unimpressed-looking mature students, and women were a minority in the department at the time. So I think we all had good reason to feel slightly uncomfortable. I have plenty of friends in academia who are gifted teachers. They bloom inside the classroom and become, for so many of their students, that teacher we've all hopefully had who inspires the route a young person elects to take in life or leaves them with a lifelong passion. These teachers take their love of the subject and transfer it to everyone in the room with a heart so open your own might almost break just looking at them. I was not that teacher. I was someone who really liked philosophy but wasn't necessarily always in the mood to talk about it with passion at nine o'clock on a Thursday morning.

Every semester, someone in the cohort of students would put their hand up when it came time to discuss philosophy of religion and say something along the lines of, 'Well I *know* that God exists.' I'd generally think *Grand so* and reply with a question like, 'Okeydokey. And what do you mean by God?' at which point the whole thing would unravel a bit and they'd leave the room forty minutes later looking distinctly less sanguine and a touch greyer than they had when they walked in. That is both the tragedy and the value of philosophy. Of asking questions generally. It unseats us. Gives us a good shake. It makes us aware of all the things we don't know and the fact that it is always vastly more than we do know.

On the second week of the first semester, a girl raised her hand neatly during a seminar and asked, 'Okay, I get that we're reading all this stuff and so on, but what's the actual *answer*?' She had the air of someone a Dungeons & Dragons nerd would describe as 'minmaxing' – trying to make optimal choices in order to maximise outcomes, arguably to the detriment of immersion and enjoyment in the process. She was being 'that guy'. In this case it seemed to me as though she was thinking about exam prep and marking break-downs. Considering how to get through this year and the ones to follow and on to a master's in public policy while reading and thinking only insofar as it would help her achieve her goals. I can understand that, but as the person contentedly trapped in a room with dead philosophers all day and who values philosophy as a discipline and a unique set of skills, I didn't exactly find the approach thrilling.

'The answer to what?' I asked, confused.

'To the mind-body problem,' the student replied.

'The *mind-body* problem?' I asked.

'Yes,' the student replied.

'*The* mind-body problem?' I asked again.

'*Yes,*' the student replied, now clearing her throat audibly.

I took a breath to calm my soaring sense of anxiety. The ensuing pause bloated like an inflating balloon to fill the classroom, lifting people out of their seats and crushing them flat to the wall.

'The mind-body problem which has been the subject of philosophical enquiry for centuries?' I asked. 'The one which interrogates whether the stuff of consciousness is physically embodied? Which has wrestled with how non-physical phenomena can arise from physical ones and which asks whether a mind is a separate entity from a brain, leading to questions bearing upon the very nature not only of the self but of our ability to know or even conceive of a reality beyond the limited bounds of human cognition?'

'Yeah. That one,' the girl replied with a slight flitter of sarcasm but nonetheless still looking mildly hopeful. Like this interaction might still go her way. The pen, which she had pointed briefly and merrily at me upon uttering the words 'that one' now floated lightly above her notebook, ready to go. Indelibly poised for answers. It had a fluffy bobble on the end that was undulating gently in the draught coming in through the gap under the door like seaweed in a placid current and I thought, not for the first time, that philosophy wasn't designed to make people sad but it might as well have been.

I think I probably blagged my way through an answer without crying like a hysterical fan unravelling at a

Taylor Swift concert or forcing the class through an impromptu PowerPoint presentation featuring everyone who has kicked the mind-body problem around since Descartes (every one of them really gave it their all, by the way). I don't remember what I told the student in response to her query but I was, as they say at home, shook. Not by the fact that we were now two weeks into the semester and this bright young person clearly hadn't yet done any of the assigned reading – that was not so unusual and I can respect a spot of shirking as much as the next shirker.

Rather, it was because she clearly saw the search for a single definitive answer as the ultimate purpose of asking a question. She appeared to believe that a question is rendered valuable, and is given meaning, only through its answer. Like something you can neatly shut the lid on and push to the dusty, spidery back recess of the under-stairs cupboard with the toe of your boot. Whatever happened to asking to ask? Wondering for the benefit of the unanticipated things that might be revealed in the process? For the other questions that might scuttle forth to spook us? I didn't blame the student – she was only reflecting the standard position on question-asking we all encounter when moving through the world. It's how we are taught to think about questions from our infancy even though little children are generally natural philosophers. They *are* the weird guy in the corner asking inappropriate questions.

A friend's kid once asked me if birds have names we'll never know because maybe birds name their babies and people can't understand bird language. Little children ask big questions. About where we come from, why we're here and why things work the way they do. Little children wonder whether someone's shadow has something in common with the person it mimics, or whether their bichon frisé Noodles feels love in the same way that they do, or why some people don't like to share even though they always want some of what you've got. The notion that questions are only valuable when there's a conclusive and readily or empirically available answer is one that philosophy either disabuses you of, or you switch courses to find a discipline where clear empirical answers will yield reasonably to proportionate effort, like engineering.

All this is to say, I suppose, that I endeavour to keep my promises. I told you back when we first got together (in the introduction) that I didn't have any answers and I'm confident that I haven't delivered a single one within the pages of this book. Instead, I've done the only thing I reliably know how to do: I've stood in a creased jacket by the table against the far wall at the birthday party, conveniently close to the bowl of glazed cocktail sausages and as far as possible from your aunt who demands to know when I'm going to get my act together and have a baby, and I've asked my silly little big questions about identity. I've considered how much of any one of us can be captured by the labels we use – and the ones we need – to make our way through the world coherently and with compassion, both for ourselves and for other people.

Couched in that long, intergenerational conversation between philosophers about the mind-body problem, by the way, there is not one definitive answer, but there is a concept called emergence. It comes from the Latin word *emergere* – a beautiful word even just to look at, it means to rise up or out, or to bring to light. There is something ethereal about the word, as though it refers to something ineffable and mysterious. Something borrowed and just out of reach. And so it does.

The concept can be traced back to our old friend John Stuart Mill, whose work has become, among other things, the tech bro and overzealous activist's handbook for remodelling society. Hammers and nails, I suppose. Still, Mill touched on the concept of emergent properties in his *A System of Logic* in 1843, when he explored the possibility that the whole may exhibit properties that cannot be deduced through the properties of its parts.

It was George Henry Lewes who first used that lovely, voluptuous term – 'emergent' – in this context, though, in his 1875 book *Problems of Life and Mind*. He suggested the difference between what he calls 'resultant' effects as opposed to 'emergent' ones. Resultant effects can be predicted solely from the sum of their parts, like green paint resulting from the combination of blue and yellow. Emergent properties are more complex. They cannot be predicted solely from the sum of their parts. They are an outcome that doesn't necessarily logically follow directly from the amalgamation of components. They are a thing that rises up, or is brought to light, unexpectedly or in ways that we cannot quite account for by looking at the parts that compose it.

It was the philosopher and scientist C. D. Broad who formalised the concept of emergence in *The Mind and Its Place in Nature* in 1925. A key part in a network of thinkers both before and after him, a network which includes both Descartes and the student with the fluffy bobble thing on the end of her pen, Broad considered the relationship between mental properties and matter. He came to the conclusion that 'an emergent property of a whole is a property that it is impossible to logically infer from even the most complete knowledge of the properties of the whole'.

It all gets a bit less beautiful (depending on your conception of beauty) after that, but for our purposes it is enough to say that your mind, your consciousness, your unique personhood-in-the-present, your 'I' – whatever you want to call it – is an emergent property. That you are an anomalous entity. Something that cannot be reliably predicted based on an understanding of the parts of which it is comprised. You are an elusive outcome despite all the conversations and the research, both material and metaphysical. You live in a body that sometimes miscalculates so that the toe of your shoe clips a step instead of clearing it and you stumble forward and look like an idiot. Yet there is also something that is you and it is immaterial. Despite all the pens lingering above all the notebooks and all the fingers held aloft over all the keyboards in all the classrooms, each in readiness to transcribe an answer that fits the space available, there remains something utterly ineffable about consciousness. About the human mind. About us.

We are not merely a combination of parts but something emergent, something that quite literally 'rises up' from the material components that comprise us. Like a miracle or a ghost or a story that is almost so impossible to believe that it sounds like someone made it up. We are something greater. More. Life might be mundane a lot of the time. It might be hard and dull. You might feel sometimes lonely or embarrassed or as though you shouldn't have eaten that fourth taco, but show me someone who isn't affected when they stop for a moment to consider that sublime idea of human consciousness and I'll show you someone for whom you should slow the car down to an *almost* total stop (for safety reasons) before you push them out into an obliging hedgerow. What more can any of us ask than that? What greater beauty or meaning is there in life than to be an anomalous, miraculous, ineffable thing that is more than the sum of its parts? To go looking for your 'self' and be so inherently complex, neurologically vast and philosophically interesting that you can't definitively find it; for all you know that it's there, and it's you.

Imagine, if you'd oblige me, all the discrete, necessary parts required to assemble an aeroplane neatly laid out on the powdery white sand of an empty beach. First, what a mess and does anyone know when the tide is coming in? This was clearly a terrible idea. But just imagine them there all the same. Every single screw and bolt needed to connect the thing together. Every panel of metal. The seats sitting in the sand, ready to be installed and looking like wide, squat people queuing patiently for a public toilet. The fuselage. Even the fuel is there, ready to be put to use as soon as there is a tank to put it in. A couple of errant wheels are nestled in an obliging dune nearby. That little oven they use to heat the terrible food is about to go out with the tide. There will be an engine knocking around here somewhere along with all the rest of it.

Now, an aeroplane is not an emergent property of these components in the philosophical sense. We know that if they are all properly assembled (before the tide comes in) and set in working order by a team of people with the relevant equipment and expertise, a working plane will eventually materialise on the beach. And yet for now, we just have components. If some moron wandered drunkenly over, pointed at the debris all over the place and roared, 'Look! A plane!' you'd hardly agree with him.

If the beach sat serenely on a desert island miles from food and civilisation and you were stranded there alone, you wouldn't fall to your knees in profound relief that you'd discovered a viable means of transport home. You'd be quite sure that what was strewn around the beach does not constitute a plane. You'd be living for the next twenty years in the shell of the fuselage. So you have components but what you absolutely do not have is an aeroplane. There is a sense in which everything – from planes to green paint to dumb guys shouting on the beach – is more than the sum of its parts.

We are a real species of rock-kickers. We love anything we can weigh and measure. We go weak at the knees for questions with answers, or rather really just for the answers. If you let us, we'll take a numerical approach to anything, even a concept like identity. For a while there, and in some circles still, questions of identity seemed limited to considering little beyond who is empowered and who is oppressed, specifically through a lens of collective identity. It was approached like a series of concentric circles with white men in the middle and various other identity labels placed based on their relationship to groups termed either oppressed or oppressor. This is not a useful, nuanced or compassionate way to approach our relationships to one another. It erases people's individuality rather than celebrating or even acknowledging it. In an attempt to acknowledge and encapsulate systemic problems, it strips individuals of their complexity. It's certainly a terrible basis upon which any of us might build our own sense of identity when in reality we are all both heroes and villains (and often something blander in the middle) within the stories that we tell ourselves in order to live.

'Show me the components,' this collectivised conception of the individual suggests, 'and I'll show you the whole. I'll show you who you are and how you are permitted to identify.' It's not a million miles away from my grandmother's old interrogative greeting, that invitation to be evaluated through a narrow sociological proxy for arithmetic – '*And who are your people?*' As though we can quantify a person's value, role and individual potential according either to who they're claimed by or lumped in with. As though we can somehow capture the whole if we just do our sums right. As though we can make sense of it all, and find the one true answer.

There's an emergent quality to life and living things which makes all of us unique. Meaningfully unique, that is. Not in a tokenistic 'sign up to my incredibly expensive vegan manifestation conference where poor people aren't allowed unless they're serving (strictly fair trade and organic) green juices for a subsistence wage' kind of way. In a real, tangible, powerful way. In a way that is legitimately true and comforting (a very rare combination) no matter where you're standing. Whether you're in the middle of the worst day of your life, standing alone in the corner of the party or surrounded by friends and family who see and value

226

your uniqueness as you see and value theirs. Whether you're exactly where you want to be in your life or sitting beneath a steady stream of tepid shower water fully clothed and weeping about your situationship. Whether you are the most confident person you know or whether you are lonely, frustrated or have spent your life until now internalising someone else's story about who you are or who you are allowed to be.

'Who am I?' is a question that only you can attempt to answer. This is because we tend to make the routine mistake of seeing other people as a conglomeration of labels. The logical product of their experience and environment. Something that can be reliably predicted from the component parts we observe (which we generally presume to be all the parts there are). We interpret them through the labels they ask us to associate with them and the ones we attribute to them because we too are products of our own experience. Because we believe we see things they don't. Only the view differs depending on who is looking.

As rock-kickers, we can be guilty of focusing too determinedly on the components. We like to pick up bits of scrap metal and accuse them of being the same thing as a plane. So here I am at the birthday party I swore blind I wasn't coming to. My jacket is creased and I'm now immersed in talking about theoretical bird language and whether a shadow is a person who lives in another dimension with some child who wandered up and thought – incorrectly – that I'm probably as trustworthy as the lollipop lady in a high-vis vest who helps everyone safely cross the road to get to school.

If you look over from where you're standing, you'll see a small, unassuming, possibly slightly starey person. A woman. If you're astute, you might discreetly lean towards your pocket and make a mark on your autistic birthday-party bingo card. Or, if you're very astute, you might not. I might look a bit sad, so you could presume either 'philosopher' or 'history of mental illness'. Honestly, in this economy I see no clean difference between the two. You may not be able to tell on sight that I'm Irish, but the signs will probably be there if you know what to look for. I won't have touched the English butter, for one thing. Unsalted? Why don't we all just, to evoke P. G. Wodehouse, hide behind the sofa and commend our souls to God?

You might see in my 'notions' sartorial choices and preference for minimalist but just-expensive-enough (for those who know how to tell) jewellery a comfortable middle-class woman or a working-class grasper who has learned what is needed to pass and signal status in circles she wasn't born into. You might see someone who is insecure performing a role, or a person just being confidently themselves over there by the cocktail sausages. Both are true. Neither gets to the heart of any of it. Neither captures that ineffable thing that rises up from the parts that comprise it. Those are some of my parts. Only some.

Acknowledgements

WRITING ABOUT YOUR OWN life is always a supremely self-indulgent act, and writing anything like a memoir under the age of forty might be an indicator of complete derangement. Still, the labels we wear are such a strange blend of the public and the personal that it was the only way I could see to write this book. I owe a tremendous debt to countless people for their help, guidance and encouragement.

My brother Damien Kennedy for mothering me in the absence of our mother, and for his forbearance when I try to mother him back. Ciara McInerney, Astrid and Thoralf for always being on my team and allowing me to play with scooters inside the house. Mary and Derek McCarthy for their support throughout my life, for stepping in when things were hardest, and for laughing heartily at me when I'm rude instead of telling me to cop on. Colm and Joan Kennedy for giving me a chance that helped me to get where I am. The whole McEvoy family for being in my life. Aoife and Daniel Crawford for making every room they are in the best place to hang out and for the deep and total support they have given me and my writing as long as I've known them (which is now a very long time).

I'm deeply grateful to my editor, Deirdre Nolan at Eriu, for her patience and support in making this book a book (with pages and everything!) rather than a vague intention I'll get round to eventually, and also to Lisa Gilmour and the teams at Eriu and Bonnier for all their help. I'm especially indebted to my agent, Catherine Cho, for her support. No one I know embodies rigorous competence, love of books and a sort of gentle interpersonal warmth in the way that she does. (I would like to be Catherine when I grow up.)

I owe more than they will ever realise to people who championed my writing at various stages of my life when they had no particular reason to – David O'Halloran and Tom Shortt for guidance, good will and good advice when I was green as a snapped twig, Professor David Berman for all the years, words, challenge, support and ideas, and for being the model of an individual in a world that pushes us to conform. Sarah Jossel for being the sort of friend and boss you don't see twice in one lifetime. Róisín Ingle for my first opportunity and for years of supportive friendship. Also for that excellent lunch in London where she convinced me that this book was worth writing. Blindboy Boatclub, whose work on autism in adulthood helped me find my own perspective on a new label. Helen Pluckrose, for seeing value in my work, for extending her liberal tolerance to putting up with me and my milky cups of tea, and for valuable advice and help in my research and thinking. Ayishat Akanbi, for her friendship and goodness, and for countless conversations that have prompted me to think more, more carefully, or better.

My thanks to Hamish McKenzie, Farrah Storr and Clyde Rathbone at Substack for support, encouragement, and welcoming me into a digital space where writers are valuable and set loose to create as they will.

I'm also deeply grateful to Sarah Maria Griffin, Simone Gannon, Julie Kirwan, Claire Coleman, Mike Sowden and Tom Cox for professional support, advice, and being generally excellent human beings. Special thanks also to Angela Kelsey, Tara Doyle, John McMillan, Bob Beverley, Shanna ní Rabhartaigh, Bernie Gibson, Shu Colwell, Niall 'Banogue' Carroll, JJ Hodari and Aoife Connolly for directly enabling me to write this book through their support.

Finally, I am grateful to J., who defies all categorisation, for his energy, his relentless intellect, for being himself in all things no matter what and for making me braver by standing beside me in all of it.